Gathering the Fragments

Other books in Cornish and about Cornwall from Evertype

A Wreck upon the Ocean (Brendan McMahon 2015)

Gooth ha Gowvreus (Jane Austen, tr. Nicholas Williams 2015)

Der an Gweder Meras ha Mys a Gafas Alys Ena (Lewis Carroll, tr. Nicholas Williams, 2015)

Aventurs Alys in Pow an Anethow (Lewis Carroll, tr. Nicholas Williams, 2015)

An Hobys, pò An Fordh Dy ha Tre Arta (J.R.R. Tolkien, tr. Nicholas Williams 2014)

An Introduction to the Laws of the Duchy of Cornwall (John Kirkhope 2014)

Geryow Gwir: The lexicon of revived Cornish (Nicholas Williams, 2014)

Tredden in Scath (Jerome K. Jerome, tr. Nicholas Williams 2014)

An Gwyns i'n Helyk (Kenneth Graham, tr. Nicholas Williams 2013)

Towards a Cornish Philosophy (Alan M. Kent 2013)

Gwerryans an Planettys (H. G. Wells, tr. Nicholas Williams 2013)

Ky Teylu Baskerville (Arthur Conan Doyle, tr. Nicholas Williams 2012)

Flehes an Hens Horn (Edith Nesbit, tr. Nicholas Williams 2012)

Desky Kernowek: A complete guide to Cornish (Nicholas Williams, 2012)

Phyllis in Piskie-land (J. Henry Harris 2012)

An Beybel Sans: The Holy Bible in Cornish (tr. Nicholas Williams 2011)

Whedhlow ha Drollys a Gernow Goth (Nigel Roberts, tr. Nicholas Williams 2011)

The Beast of Bodmin Moor: Best Goon Brèn (Alan Kent, tr. Neil Kennedy 2011)

Enys Tresour (Robert Louis Stevenson, tr. Nicholas Williams 2010)

Whedhlow Kernowek: Stories in Cornish (A.S.D. Smith, ed. Nicholas Williams 2010)

Henry Jenner's Handbook of the Cornish Language (ed. Michael Everson 2010)

The Cult of Relics: Devocyon dhe Greryow (Alan Kent, tr. Nicholas Williams, 2010)

Jowal Lethesow: Whedhel a'm West a Gernow (Craig Weatherhill, tr. Nicholas Williams, 2009)

Skeul an Tavas: A coursebook in Standard Cornish (Ray Chubb, 2009)

Kensa Lyver Redya (Harriette Treadwell & Margaret Free, tr. Eddie Foirbeis Climo, 2009)

Adro dhe'n Bÿs in Peswar Ugans Dëdh (Jules Verne, abridged and tr. Kaspar Hocking, 2009)

A Concise Dictionary of Cornish Place-Names (Craig Weatherhill, 2009)

Form and Content in Revived Cornish (Everson, Weatherhill, Chubb, Deacon, Williams, 2006)

Towards Authentic Cornish (Nicholas Williams, 2006)

Writings on Revived Cornish (Nicholas Williams, 2006)

Cornish Today (Nicholas Williams, 2006)

Gathering the Fragments

Storytelling and Cultural Resistance in Cornwall

Brendan McMahon

evertype
2016

Published by Evertype, 73 Woodgrove, Portlaoise, Ireland. *www.evertype.com*.

Text © 2016 Brendan McMahon.
Foreword © 2016 Alan M. Kent.

First edition 2016.

A catalogue record for this book is available from the British Library.

ISBN-10 1-78201-168-4
ISBN-13 978-1-78201-168-2

Typeset in Baskerville by Michael Everson.

Cover design by Michael Everson, based on "A Gatherer of Winkles and Limpets" by Clifton Johnson, *The Isle of the Shamrock* (1901).

Printed and bound by LightningSource.

Contents

Acknowledgements

With thanks to the editor of *An Baner Kernewek* and the British Journal of Psychotherapy in which some of this material first appeared.

Thanks also to Owen McKnight and Emma Jones at the Celtic Library, Jesus College Oxford for their help.

To Joe.

Foreword

Should Cornwall ever—in some imaginary world of the future— have a fully developed "Cornu-centric" University that offers a Celtic Studies programme, then this fine new volume by Brendan McMahon would instantly quality as being on the reading list of both undergraduate and postgraduate courses. Bookending neatly into another recent volume of his, *A Wreck Upon the Ocean: Cornish Folklore in the Age of the Industrial Revolution* (2015), the subject matter here specifically, is the nature of storytelling in Cornwall, and how that endeavour has acted, over the centuries, as a piece of cultural resistance into incorporation into an English colonial project.

The material assembled here shows, in various genres and oeuvres how the Cornish have steadfastly maintained their cultural identity. The volume also subjects these moments of narrative to McMahon's own speciality: psychology, examining how these "story" components of Cornwall's past have been formed in the mind, and why they have been important for Cornish people. In so doing, McMahon adroitly crosses many boundaries: literary studies, oral narrative, folklore, history, ethno-nationalism, and of course, psychology itself. The hybridity of this endeavour is its best feature since the author is able to seamlessly interconnect these aspects, whilst maintaining a view of Cornwall's specific historical experience.

McMahon's concept of a "storied world" introduces the reader to the imaginative constructs operating in Cornwall, and the reader is then lead through aspects of this: visiting initially the classic corpus of Cornish literature texts, but valuably reinterpreting them along story lines. There is, for example a fascinating piece of fifteenth-century text from the "Red Book of Bath", referring to an Arthurian Cornwall, as well as exploration of the cultural shifts that occurred when the oral tradition stopped being oral and became "frozen" in text. The key motif of memory helps us to unfold and deliver the narrative, since it is so securely linked to people's own cultural geography and take on the world. Lurking deep within this is our populist theatrical tradition, and the author leads us to new appreciations of the corpus, as well as appraisals of pieces newly discovered text such as *Bewnans Ke / The Life of St Kea*. Folkloristic and cultural symbols are also examined as important markers of Cornish identity and long-held resistance. In this capacity, McMahon links to wider pan-British and pan-European movements, connecting—let us be honest—the incredible tenacity of the Cornish Revival with other Romantic, Folkloric and Literary moments.

The volume also deeply links the storytelling of the Cornish with their European identity as a Celtic people of Europe. Again, here McMahon shows how narratives have travelled and been re-imagined in different contexts. A central tenet of the argument is how these stories get retold and recycled for different generations—and for different cultural purposes. The unconscious and conscious parts of our minds help us to form and regulate this process of recapitulating the past. With adept ease, McMahon is also able to link these processes to the theories of Sigmund Freud, Carl Jung and Walter Benjamin.

Later in the work, there is a new look at Anglo-Cornish fiction over the years, and how this genre has imagined "storied" Cornwall. Not only is there a reconsideration of now established authors and texts, but also investigations into some texts that readers will know little about (Amy Clarke's *Roskelly of Roskelly* comes to mind) and which deserve more study. I was obviously pleased to see McMahon's further reflections on those most successful of Anglo-Cornish novelists, Silas and Joseph Hocking, who dominated Britain's view of Cornwall in the late nineteenth and early twentieth century. Alongside this, classic texts, such as Edward Bosanketh's Tin, Walter Besant's *Armorel of Lyonesse* and Wilkie Collins' *Rambles Beyond Railways* are examined again, in the light of the author's findings. The topic of exile in fiction is also given scrutiny and this proves to be a fruitful area, since this is so much a part of the Cornish experience both in the past and in the present. Oral narrative also transferred (as I have seen first hand), to the mining landscapes of North America, Australia and New Zealand. After consideration of these narratives, the volume concludes with reflections once again on the Cornish capacity for "droll-telling".

The title of this volume refers to a familiar adage, most often applied on the early revival in Cornwall. Although, it may, through a certain lens, almost be a lament; through another, it is very positive. It suggests firstly, that despite globalization, and the encroachment of English culture and media, the fragments exist. They have not fully disappeared. Secondly, of course, it suggests, that we are able to collect and identity them, and understand how they fit into Cornwall's unique history. Finally, as McMahon seems to suggest here, if we have enough of them, the very vase (or as Cornu-English might put it, "buzza") that was once cracked and broken, can be rebuilt and reassembled. There may be a few cracks but the original culture stands proudly before us.

While we may have once mistakenly thought that Cornwall was "scat to lerrups", and simply not repairable, the reverse is the case. Not only is Cornwall gathering the fragments, but as well as now leading innovation in the discipline of Celtic Studies, it is also confidently and assuredly putting things back together again. McMahon shows us how.

Alan M. Kent
Probus, Beltane 2016

Introduction

"Gather up the fragments that remain, that nothing be lost."

John 6:12

The Storied World

This book is predicated on the importance of storytelling. We use stories to make sense of our lives and our world, and of our place in the world, where we came from and where we might be going. This works on several levels. When we have to introduce ourselves to other people, we tell them a story about ourselves, which might or might not resemble the stories we use to explain ourselves to ourselves. These stories deal with personal experience, though they also incorporate historical and cultural experience, such as family background or migration for instance; though this narrative is of course deeply personal, it also indicates where our experience might intersect with others, and when we meet strangers for instance we usually try to find common ground.

These internal narratives define who we are. Like mirrors, they present us with images in which we can recognize ourselves. Stories of the type collected by Hunt and Bottrell can also help us to deal with the developmental issues which we face growing up and these issues were explored in my earlier book.[1] But stories can also provide a foundation for whole communities, especially if they are shared in a communal setting, like the big narrative of the "divine economy" in the *Ordinalia* for instance, embodying the faith of the Cornish people which linked them with the rest of Europe. In such contexts, as in the droll telling tradition, storytelling becomes a "rite of memory" connecting individuals with each other and their collective

---

1 McMahon, B. (2015). *A Wreck upon the Ocean: Cornish Folklore in the Age of the Industrial Revolution*. Portlaoise, Evertype.

part, in an affirmation of faith in the future. At the same time the publication of forgotten texts in the Cornish language is also an act of memory, making possible serious attempts to revive Cornish as a spoken language, and feeding into the nationalist movements which began to emerge at the end of the nineteenth century, since language is one sign of nationhood. Folk tales moved from oral tradition to text, at the precise point when they were facing extinction, and we shall be exploring these parallels in the wider context of Victorian Britain.

Both Cornwall and Victorian Britain underwent unprecedented change during the course of the nineteenth century. The large scale mining of copper and tin changed the physical environment, and the economic crisis from the 1870s on increased the pace of emigration to a flood. The traditional way of life of Cornish fishing and farming people changed forever. Cornwall became more integrated into the British state as communications improved, and its traditional distinctiveness was seen in a negative light, except insofar as it could be used to construct a new identity as a tourist destination. Britain also changed due to industrialization and ideological shifts. In Cornwall Methodism provided a new religious narrative while, despite parallel developments elsewhere, such as the influential Oxford Movement, religious faith came under attack from positivism and evolutionary theory and the increasing rationalism and scepticism of the times. These uncertainties combined with racism and confidence in their own achievements to produce a tendency to expropriate, a tendency which included overseas territory and the natural world (including the natural resources of Cornwall, for instance), and a strong need to classify and catalogue what they found. This was of course a function of imperialism and the need to accumulate capital, against a background of increasing international competition. All of this helps to make sense of Victorian attitudes toward Cornish folklore and literature.

Both British and Cornish culture were changing rapidly in a world which was transformed and permeated by loss. In response to this desperate attempts were made to save what remained of the past, to preserve and classify it. In the British context this was also a process of appropriation. Knowledge and even the past itself, was a commodity to be acquired, and the acquisition of territory overseas was paralleled by the acquisition of knowledge, both scientific and cultural, at home. Indeed the two were often part of the same process, as historic and biological loot poured into Kew and the British Museum from all corners of the globe. On the intellectual side this process permeated all disciplines, including the newly emergent sciences of archaeology, philology and Celtic Studies, all of which were shaped by the dominant interests of the age, and which therefore are marked by the ambivalence and anxiety of the time. Archaeology, by appropriating and categorizing the past, becomes a metaphor for the process, which is also exemplified in the collection and publication of Cornish folklore and literature. In their original versions both these art forms served as rites of memory, mirrors to reflect the Cornish people to itself. From this point, they become commodities and serve the wider imperial project, their radical potential disguised and denied.

The Novel

The most characteristic form of Victorian literature was the novel, which gives us much of the best sense of how Victorians lived their lives, and how they thought and felt. If we want to understand the religious crisis, for instance, we need to read Mrs Humphrey Ward's *Robert Elsmere*, or John Henry Newman's *Loss and Gain*.[2] The boom in the circulating libraries met the needs of an expanding middle-class readership, though the popularity of the three volume novel deterred working-class readers until later in the century.[3] The late eighteenth-century Gothic craze for stories such as Mrs Radcliffe's "The Mysteries of Udolpho" eventually succumbed to bourgeois realism, but it also fed into the "sensation novel, as written by Wilkie Collins and Mrs Braddon, which enjoyed an immense vogue in the 1840s. Popular fiction often gives an unconscious reflection of the issues which preoccupy readers, and this was particularly true in Victorian times, when Gothic fantasy allowed for the expression of

2 Ward, Mary Augusta (1888). Robert Elsmere, London. Newman, J. H. (1848). *Loss and Gain*. Reprinted 1986, Oxford University Press.

3 See Neuburg, V. E. (1977). *Literature: A History and Guide from the Beginning of Printing to the Year 1897*. Pp. 149-151. Harmondsworth Penguin.

unconscious anxieties, as in the paintings of Richard Dadds, for instance;[4] and the Victorians had plenty to be anxious about. Cornish writers, whether consciously or not, used the genre to explore Cornwall's particular dilemmas, and possible responses to them: one result of this was the so-called "pulp Methodism" of the Hocking brothers.[5] In less ideological novels, such as those of Amy Clarke, we see a less self-conscious reflection of Cornishness. There are plenty of novels with a Cornish setting which have no distinctive sense of Cornishness at all, but even they may tell us something of how Cornwall is understood, or misunderstood, across the Tamar. Wilkie Collins' travelogue of 1850, *Rambles Beyond Railways* is particularly informative. Though there is no link between the "Cornish novels" on the one hand and Cornish language texts on the other, there is a link between novels and folklore, and the Hocking novels for instance are full of folkloristic references, as indeed is Amy Clarke's *Roskelly of Roskelly*, of which more later. And her book, however distanced from the tradition, has a "rite of memory" at its heart.

I have made extensive use of Cornish literature here because it is the clearest Cornish voice we have, the last voice of a Cornwall that could speak clearly for itself in its own tongue. After that it becomes harder for Cornwall to speak, as its institutions, language and connections with the wider world are destroyed and it becomes, for a while at least, a provincial English backwater, before acquiring a new industrial, then post-industrial identity; and the nineteenth century novel helps us to understand this process. Joseph Pearce's stories also help us to understand the mood at the end of the century.

Cornish Celts

If culture is a mirror within which we can see our reflection, past, present and future, then migration, the immediate tragic con-sequences of which are very much with us as I write this, also presents a threat to identity. For those who remain, the prospect of assimilation presents a rather different threat. For Cornwall in the

4 See Dadds' *"The Fairy Feller's Master Stroke"*. Tate, London, 1855-64.
5 See Kent, Alan M. (2000). *The Literature of Cornwall*. Bristol, Redcliffe Press, pp. 160-5.

twentieth century the wider Celtic identity seemed to offer an answer, especially given its relative success in Wales and especially Ireland.[6] This wider sense of identity had a long life and inspired such activism on behalf of the "Celtic" nations and their cultures, not least through the pancelticism of the Celtic League,[7] but in reality the "Celtic" peoples had never shown much solidarity, and the idea had perhaps more appeal in the smaller nations or in England than elsewhere: the first Cornish language novel espoused panceltic views.[8] Other short novels in Cornish have been written since then, but a wider language revival seems necessary for the literature to gain ground.

A further problem with pancelticism was the instability of the term "Celtic",[9] which seems to have acquired its modern connotations towards the end of the nineteenth century. There is in fact no real evidence for large scale Celtic immigration to the British Isles. The Victorians tended to see history in terms of invasion, conquest, and occupation, because this was the model they applied in their own world, and the theory that "'twas ever thus" provided them with some justification. Much as we would like to believe that history, and for that matter science, are objective pursuits, that the past cannot be altered, the fact is that we see the past through the eyes of the present. Andrew Wawn has brilliantly shown how the "old north" of Viking days was shaped by a Victorian agenda, and Celtic history was similarly shaped.[10] In part this is based on racist assumptions of course, but it also owed something to Carlyle's famous dictum that "might is right":

> Might was right because in (God's) universe only what was right was given the strength to succeed. True, injustice might

6 Deacon, B. *et al.* (2003). *Mebyan Kernow and Cornish Nationalism*. Cardiff, Welsh Academic Press.
7 Berresford Ellis, P. (1985). *The Celtic Revolution: A Study in Anti-Imperialism*. Tallybont, Y Lolfa.
8 Bennetto, M. (1984). *An Gurun Wosek A Geltya: The Bloody Crown of the Celtic Countries*. Redruth, Dylansow Truran.
9 Chapman, M. (1992). *The Celts: The Construction of a Myth*. London, Macmillan.
10 Wawn, A. (2000). *The Vikings and the Victorians: Inventing the Old North in Nineteenth Century Britain*. Cambridge, D. S. Brewer, pp. 30-34.

have power enough to conquer temporarily, but in the long run the victory of strength was bound to be the victory of justice. But for how long? Carlyle did not say, One might jump the gun, perhaps, and conclude at once that the side of power was the side of God and the use of force the legitimate weapon against whatever obstructed one's "just" desires. The doctrine that might is right when the might is just can slide with fatal ease into the belief that might is— right. Or with equal ease, a man's personal desire can be identified with justice.[11]

This appalling, indeed blasphemous view was of some use in justifying dreadful things for which there was absolutely no moral justification. Carlyle himself for instance justified the opium wars thus:

Our friends of China, who guiltily refused to trade... had we not to argue with them, in cannon-shot at last, and convince them that they ought to trade![12]

This world view had a formative influence on Celtic Studies as it developed in the course of the nineteenth century. It was widely believed that the Celtic languages were brought to western Europe and the British Isles by a wave of invasions during the Iron Age, originating in central Europe and associated with the peoples of the great archaeological sites of Hallstatt and La Tène. Victorian books had maps with huge black arrows illustrating this process, rather resembling those illustrating Hitler's Panzer divisions in the Blitzkrieg. It has been known for some time that this didn't happen in reality. Of course the Victorians cannot be blamed for not knowing what was not yet known, but we do need to take their world-view into account in evaluating their huge achievements. We also need to understand our own world view, or we too will misinterpret what we see. None of this means that the Cornish are

11 Houghton, W. E. (195710. *The Victorian Frame of Mind.* New Haven, Yale University Press, p. 215.
12 *Ibid.*, p. 209.

not Celts who speak or once spoke a Celtic language (the term can only accurately be applied to languages), only that they are not descended from tall, blond warriors who once conquered a short, dark aboriginal people and imposed their language upon them: this is a Victorian English narrative, and there is no trace of it in the Cornish tradition.

The current debate about the Tartessian language seems to bear this out.[13] Tartessian was a language once spoken in southern Iberia, surviving in inscriptions dated 750 BCE to 350 BCE, only ninety-seven of which survive. If the language is indeed Celtic, and the paucity of material makes it difficult to be sure, then it is the earliest attested Celtic language. It certainly seems to resemble other early languages such as Gaulish and Celtiberian, once spoken in eastern Spain.

The early dates for the inscriptions render the invasion hypothesis impossible, such that we can no longer:

> ... assume that the Celtic language must have originated in the same time and place as the Hallstatt and La Tène cultures. In fact a shift in focus from Iron Age central Europe to the Atlantic Bronge Age is indicated as the more meaningful starting place for a new narrative story of the Celts... The proposed paradigm shift would affect how we understand early Britain in a number of ways. Not only would Britain have become Celtic, in the sense of Celtic speaking, at an earlier date than usually allowed, but probably by different mechanisms and possibly from a different direction.[14]

That is, the Celtic languages evolved from Indo-European in the west, and were not imposed by fire and sword. There were no huge black arrows.

---

13 Koch, J. T. (2013). *Tartessian: Celtic in the South-West at the Dawn of History* (2nd edition). Aberystwyth, Celtic Studies Publications.
14 *Ibid.*, p. 271.

INTRODUCTION

The Unconscious Mind

It is hard to say how conscious the Victorians were of their own ambivalence, the contrast between their destructiveness and a creative energy that bordered on the astonishing. No doubt Marxists would say that it was the inevitable result of early capitalism, the need to acquire resources to beat the competition. But it included an intellectual acquisitiveness that seems to be more emotionally driven. Certainly many writers worried about "the condition of England", and Dickens' later novels, for instance portrayed the country as a dank prison. For all their achievements and surface optimism, Victorians worried. They built workhouses to contain the poor, and commissioners' churches to deter them from resolution, but still Chartism and the French Revolution cast long shadows down the century.[15] Evangelical Puritanism, which was not confined to the dissenting sects, made many lives a misery, and what many saw as the scientific challenge to religion produced a widespread sense of insecurity.[16] Financial instability combined with a new social mobility to provoke anxiety about social status and the fear of losing it, which haunts many Victorian novels.

Freud's great psychoanalytic project began in 1880 with his analysis of Anna O. He learned much from Charcot at the Salpetriere in Paris and began to publish papers, including his *Studies on Hysteria* in 1895.[17] In 1900 his great "dream" book, *The Interpretation of Dreams* was published, in which he theorized that dreams can express underlying psychological conflicts which give rise to neurotic illnesses such as anxiety and depression. Psychoanalysis offered a way of understanding and resolving such conflicts. It also offered a way of interpreting, and sometimes explaining away culture, as in his papers on Michelangelo, and Leonardo da Vinci, in which his interpretation depends on what turns out to be a mistranslation.[18] In this respect perhaps psycho-

15 Checkland, S. G. and E. O. A. (1974). *The Poor Law Report of 1834*. London, Pelican. And Curl, J S (2000). *Oxford Dictionary of Architecture*. Oxford, OUP, p. 189.
16 Houghton, *op. cit.*, pp. 54-89.
17 See Gay, P. (1988). *Freud: A Life for our Time*. London, Papermac. And Gay, P. (1995). *The Freud Reader*. London, Vintage, pp. 48-111.
18 For these and related writings see Freud, S. (1985). *Art and Literature*. Penguin

analysis was part of a European impulse towards intellectual hegemony, a desire to master the world through knowledge, analogous in some respects to archaeology and the mastery and classification of dead languages. Freud himself was aware of this analogy and kept archaeological artefacts on his desk. On the other hand psychoanalysis deflated bourgeois confidence by drawing attention to the aggression and desire which lurked beneath the surface. Many of the characteristic habits of thought at that time, such as racism, "might is right", and related attitudes towards the Cornish, were defence mechanisms designed to protect the Victorians from the knowledge of what they were doing, from seeing themselves as they actually were. Freud's work therefore was an imperialist attempt to colonize the unconscious mind, the last frontier, but simultaneously a subversive, Bohemian assault on middle-class morality.

In his short 1919 paper "The Uncanny" ("Das Unheimlich"), Freud discusses this feeling, which was an important component of both contemporary supernatural fiction and the folktale.[19] Ghost stories are popular in the oral tradition (the "Tregeagle" stories in Cornwall, for instance), but literary ghost stories were largely a Victorian creation, forming a counterbalance to secularism and nationalism. Freud explains both in terms of repressed infantile memories which return in adult life provoking anxiety.

No doubt this does contribute something to our understanding of the stories concerned. But it doesn't really explain why people tell the stories (to revive buried infantile anxieties?) and it ignores the social context entirely. It privileges the psychoanalytic narrative at the expense of the popular one, and it puts the psychoanalyst himself in a position of power: he is judge and jury and will decide what the story really means, whatever storyteller and audience think it means. In this he is entirely representative of the nineteenth-century man of science. Most crucially, this approach ignores the social context: why was this story told when it was and in that particular place? Certainly folk tales are true representations of how people work psychologically

Freud Library, Vol 14. London, Penguin.

19 Freud, S. (1955). *The Uncanny*. Standard Edition Vol 17. London, Hogarth Press and The Institute of Psychoanalysis.

and emotionally, otherwise they would hardly be told. Freud embodies the Victorian desire to explain and classify everything, including desire itself. Like Mr Casauhon in George Eliot's *Middlemarch*, he provides a "key to all anthologies".

From Tale to Text
Puritanism increased the force of repression, and the tendency to judge in others the impulses one feared in oneself, whether they were there or not. This attitude influenced the transmission of stories in the working class oral tradition into print, for a new middle-class audience, especially as the working class, along with women and foreigners, were suspected of harbouring unruly desires. Hunt, who showed a rather unusual respect for his material, tells us that

> All the stories given in these volumes are the genuine household tales of the people. The only liberties which have been taken with them has been to alter them from the vernacular—in which they were for the most part related—into modern language.[20]

Though Bottrell, many of whose stories were used by Hunt, says:

> In most cases the stories are given as related by the droll-tellers, except where our local dialect might be unintelligible to the general reader, or when (as is frequently the case) they indulge in a plainness of speech which the fastidious might regard as indelicate. On this account it becomes necessary to curtail and alter some stories in order to make them presentable.[21]

Many of the early collections were based on stories gathered by middle class "correspondents" which were then submitted to a final editing process, so being at two removes from the original narrative.

20 Hunt, R. (1881) 3rd edition. *Popular Romances of the West of England, or, The Drolls Traditions and Superstitions of Old Cornwall.* London, Chatto and Windus, p. 31.
21 Bottrell, W. (1870), reprinted 1996. *Traditions and Hearthside Stories of West Cornwall.* 1st series. Fecinfacce Llanerck, p. v.

The recent publication of the first edition of the Grimm Brothers' collection shows how stories can be modified by "popular", i.e. middle-class, taste, even after initial publication:

> Wilhelm could not control his desire to make the tales more artistic to appeal to middle-class reading audiences. The result is that the essence of the tales is more vivid in the two volumes of the first edition, for it is here that the Grimms made the greatest effort to respect the voices of the original storytellers or collectors.[22]

By the time they reach us the stories have been carefully filtered in the interests of propriety, and their textual history tells us as much about the contemporary world as it does about their origins.

And not only propriety. Quoting Richter and Merkel's German paper, Jack Zipes reminds us:

> The domination of the bourgeoisie and the socialisation process which developed since the eighteenth century contributed to organising and controlling the imagination of all segments of society, thereby preventing its emancipatory potential from being realised, whether in action or in art forms. To illustrate this point, they study the function of imaginative elements in the folktale and show how they underwent a decisive change when the bourgeoisie began consciously to control their transmission in books and magazines.[23]

This is why we need to understand the wider context in order to understand the stories in the form in which they have come down to us. There are certainly implied sexual relationships in the Cornish stories, in the tales of Cherry of Zennor and Anne Jefferies for instance; and emancipatory implications in the giant stories, such as

22 Zipes, J. (ed and trans) (2014) *The Original Folk and Fairy Tales of the Brothers Grimm: The Complete First Edition*. Princetown University Press, pp. xx–xxi.
23 Zipes, J. (2002 revised edition). *Breaking the Magic Spell: Radical Theories of Folk and Fairy Tales*. Lexington, University of Kentucky, p. 33.

"Jack and the Tinkeard", and whether these implications have been watered down by Hunt and Bottrell is hard to say. In any case, it seems likely that some storytellers self-censored in the presence of outsiders, and some collectors' accounts imply as much, especially as minority cultures became more self-conscious as the tradition petered out.

The Rite of Memory

But it is not simply a matter of what the stories contain. A central theme of Cornish culture is the act of shared memory itself. The medieval drama was a communal act, a shared experience of the faith which the Cornish community held in common with the rest of Europe. The experience of storytelling by the hearthside was a sharing of memory—memory of the stories they have in common, the stories which shaped the landscape in which they lived. It is as if their memory was a mirror in which they could see themselves, blurred perhaps by outside forces beyond their control, but still recognizable and true to itself. The language revival too, painful and difficult as it has been, has been an attempt to recapture an identity, a memory of the self which was nearly lost.

Chapter 1

Memory and Narrative

The Folktale

In 1829 Robert Hunt began working on his historic collection of
Cornish folktales, the first fieldwork collection of its time. As his work
progressed he also used material collected by William Bottrell. The
two collectors discovered the tradition of "droll-telling", which was
dying out in their day.[24] Though Hunt and Bottrell wandered
extensively through west Cornwall gathering their stories from the
mining, fishing and farming communities they have little to tell us
about the traditional settings in which the stories were told, either
because the nexus between storyteller and audience had already
been broken, and all that remained was a random assortment of
narrative fragments; or because such traditional story telling as
survived took place in secret, away from the critical and perhaps
mocking gaze of outsiders. But the tradition was clearly in decline,
as Bottrell says:

> In a very few years these interesting traditions would have
> been lost, unless they had been preserved in some such form
> as the present volume is intended to supply; since modern
> customs, and the diffusion of the local news of the day, are
> superseding, in even the most remote districts, the semi-
> professional droll-tellers who were formerly welcomed at all
> firesides, fairs and feasts for their recitals of the old ballads
> and stories in which they abounded, and of which their
> audiences rarely tired.[25]

---

24 The "droll" was a long, episodic tale told by itinerant storytellers, often adapted
    to fit local situations. From *drolla*, Cornish for 'story'.
25 Bottrell, *op. cit.*, pp. v-vi.

More tellingly, Hunt speaks of collecting "the old stories of which the people were beginning to be ashamed", though he too evokes a sociable hearthside setting "in close companionship with the homely miner".[26]

Both writers describe storytelling as a shared, communal experience. Bottrell's description particularly suggests a certain conviviality in the original setting which must often have been absent from the collector's encounter with the informant, though the fact that informants were "beginning to be ashamed" of their stories suggests a culture which had become demoralized as a result of prolonged dominance by a powerful, alien culture and which had lost all the institutions which had previously sustained it, particularly of course its language.

For a clearer picture of the *mise en scène* we may turn to Ireland, where the storytelling tradition is better documented. Zimmerman has identified several storytelling contexts, based on the reports of his informants, divided into two main categories:

1. Storytelling away from home, ie at work, or "to shorten the road"; and
2. Storytelling at the fireside, family gatherings and "courting".[27]

This recalls Bottrell's "hearthside" stories, and includes the famous "ceilidh", when people would visit each others' homes on a winter's night to socialize, sing and tell stories.

Arensberg and Kimball described a house-party in County Clare in the 1930s:

> the old men of the district drop in on neighbours and "friends" to sit around the hearth together, passing the evenings of winter in conversation, singing, discussing the news, and telling the old stories of legend and folklore. At the "cuaird" (visit) younger men and women, if they attend, sit behind, usually leaving the centre of the stage to the old

---

26 Hunt, *op. cit.*, p. 25.
27 Zimmerman, G. D. (2001). *The Irish Storyteller*. Dublin, Four Courts Press, pp. 453-5.

men, and the children stand up in silent admiration. The younger men have their own pursuits, of course, though at present the divergence may be more noticed than formerly.[28]

This divide by age seems to reflect cultural discontinuity, and may suggest language loss and the growing marginalization of traditional culture: one can imagine that similar forces were at work in early nineteenth-century Cornwall.

Of course, the conditions within which we encounter a story will help shape our response to it. When we read one of Hunt or Bottrell's stories today we must remember that it has already gone through a number of transpositions, from the oral tradition to the printed page, from the informant's vernacular to the received standard English of the collector, from a social setting to a solitary one, and probably from Cornish into English at some stage, quite apart from all the social and cultural shifts which separate our world from that of the storytellers and their audience.[29] It is no doubt impossible for us to unpeel all these skins and penetrate to some hypothetical original "meaning" which the story may contain, any more than we can now watch a play of Shakespeare's through Elizabethan eyes. But we do need to make an imaginative effort, otherwise we will privilege our own impoverished worldview and perpetuate the oppressive and dismissive system of thought which destroyed traditional Cornish culture in the first place. Readers are not neutral, and between audience and text, whether written or spoken, something is inevitably enacted.

These convivial gatherings clearly performed a number of functions for the people involved. The need to share information and opinion, to interact with and relate to others is constant, though the media may change. The need for entertainment "to shorten the road" also persists. But what specific needs were met by the storytelling aspects of these meetings?

And what were the stories about? Hunt gives a useful classification at the beginning of his *Popular Romances*, under the overarching

---

28 Arensberg, C. M. and Kimball, S. T. (1940). *Family and Community in Ireland*, p. 131. Cited in Zimmerman, *ibid*.

29 It has also been bowdlerized.

categories of "Romances and superstitions of the mythic ages", that is, stories about giants, fairies, mermaids, rocks, demons and lost cities; and "Romances and superstitions of historic times", which includes legends about the saints and holy wells, King Arthur and traditions of the mining and fishing industries.[30] Bottrell does not classify his stories. Whether these categories reflect real distinctions in the mind of droll teller and audience is not clear: certainly some stories seem to incorporate material from different categories, and it is unlikely that the distinctions were as clear in Cornwall as they were in early Ireland, with its tales of voyages, youthful exploits, elopements and so on.[31] It must of course also be remembered that vast amounts of material must have already been lost before the collectors began their work, due to early industrialization and the loss of the Cornish language.

Though the distinction between "mythic ages" and "historic times" suggests Victorian historicism of the kind which bedevilled contemporary religious controversy rather than the values of traditional communities, Hunt's categories are interesting. Legends of the saints and wells would have reminded listeners of their local topography, explaining the names and origins of the places they lived and worshipped in and the surrounding countryside.[32] Stories of mining and fishing would emphasize the shared life of the community, and stories of King Arthur their historical origins, and perhaps the old dream of independence, or at least the memory of it. Told at "firesides", fairs and feasts, such stories can only have reinforced the group identity of the audience by reminding them of what they were and where they came from: that is to say, such occasions functioned as a cultural mirror. At a time when their cultural identity was under threat,[33] this must have bound the group

30 Hunt, *op. cit.*
31 See Rees, A. and Rees, B. (1961) *Celtic Heritage: Ancient Tradition in Ireland and Wales. Part Three: The Meaning of Story.* London, Thames and Hudson, pp. 207-341.
32 Like the "dindshenchas" of ancient Ireland. See McKillop, C. J. (1998). *Dictionary of Celtic Mythology.* Oxford, Oxford University Press.
33 Both Hunt and Bottrell mention this as a major factor in their desire to collect the stories: "Romances such as these have floated down to us as a wreck upon the ocean. We gather a fragment here and a fragment there... and obtain a

together and helped it to survive in the face of huge social and economic change, not least mass emigration.

All this is fairly easy to understand. The fiction of the mythic stories is perhaps less so. The giant tales too have a topographical dimension, explaining how prominent features of the rocky coast were originally the giants' caves, coffins, graves and so on. Incorporating landscape into story, a story in which local people themselves participate, creates a unified world which they can understand and in which they feel they belong. The alienation from the natural world, for which it sought solace in the growing tourist industry in Cornwall following the development of the railways in the 1850s, was beginning to trouble Victorian England. The giants symbolize the powerful instinctive forces within each of us, the desire and aggression which we must all learn to manage, both individually and in communities. The stories also link us to an unimaginable ancient past, a mythic time before history, which is where Hunt places them.[34] In this sense they are creation myths, explanations of how the world came to be the way it is. Such stories also help us to locate ourselves in the place where we belong, and understand our relation to that place, not in any simplistic way, but in a way which makes imaginative, emotional sense—as well as underlining the continuity of communal existence in the same place.

Fairy stories work rather differently. Originally rooted in a cult of the dead the Cornish stories helped people to cope with anxieties about death, anxieties which are, of course, universal, but which were particularly prominent in the historic experience of Cornish people at this time, not least because of the dreadful mortality rates in the mining and fishing industries. In May 1853 for instance, one issue of *The West Briton* recorded the deaths of thirteen miners at Rotallak ("and several widows and from thirty to forty children were left destitute of the means of subsistence") and other deaths at Penhalls, Tolvadden, St Just and Wheal Buller.[35]

Such events were not uncommon, and must have had a profound impact on small communities, and combined with high infant

---

shadowy image of the people who have persisted." Hunt, *op. cit.*, p. 32.

34 See McMahon, *op. cit.*

35 Barton, R. M. (1972). *Life in Cornwall in the Late Nineteenth Century*. Truro, D. Bradford Barton.

mortality and emigration, the sense of loss must have been constantly palpable: stories of changelings, lost children, visits to the land of the dead, fairy funerals, of Cherry of Zennor and poor Anne Jeffries pining for their lost fairy lovers, helped people to deal with it. In a group setting individual loss can be shared, the sense of isolation diminishes and the community comes together to care for its own, to share the memories and assert its distinctiveness. This model of relatedness was under threat throughout Britain, but in Cornwall secularization and industrial exploitation had a colonialist edge not found elsewhere outside the Celtic fringe. These forces did in the end provoke resistance in the form of support for alternative political strategies,[36] and eventually an indigenous national movement, both preceded by cultural revival and the rediscovery of the Cornish language.

Cornish drama: The *Ordinalia*

In this sense too shared memory can reinforce identity, and what we see in the mirror is what we are. This is of course one of the functions of both language and literature, and Cornwall had lost its literature long before the nineteenth century.[37] For most of us the word "literature" conjures up the image of a shelf of books, even if in reality it takes the form of computer downloads. The word is also used to signify serious texts, which have something important to say about the business of living, as distinct from mere entertainment: "stories for the road". Neither of these distinctions is entirely valid for what survives of Cornish literature (the plays can be both funny and serious), though most of it is grounded in the "big narratives" of salvation history, and has much to say about the human condition. Most of it consists of play texts, drama written for public performance in the open-air theatres that once dotted the Cornish countryside, and not for scholarly reading in the study.[38]

36 Tregidga, G. (2012). "A Shrewd Choice: Isaac Foot and Cornish Politics in the General Election of 1910." In Payton, P. (ed), (2012). *Cornish Studies* 20.

37 Its major texts were to be published in the course of that century, the *Ordinalia* in 1850, *Pascon agan Arluth* in 1860-1, *Beunans Meriasek* in 1872. See Murdoch, B. (1993). *Cornish Literature.* Cambridge, D. S. Brewer, pp. 152-156.

38 Examples of the *plen an gwary*, 'playing places', survive at St Just in Penwith and Perran Round. See Kent, Alan M. (2010) *The Theatre of Cornwall: Space, Place,*

A translation of the Bible into Cornish in early modern times might have helped to save the language. That a medieval Cornish Bible did exist though cannot now be doubted. It was the work of John Trevisa in the 1370s and a copy did exist in the Bodleian in 1612— perhaps it still does.[39] The Bible certainly did inform such medieval Cornish as has come down to us. But that it never became an accessible printed text is a tragedy.

Before examining the plays in more detail it is important to be clear about what the *Ordinalia* is not, ie a clumsy imitation of foreign models, the amateurish product of a marginal and second-rate culture, as it is often described. Brian Murdoch tells us:

> The three plays known as the *Ordinalia* are the high point of medieval Cornish literature, the point at which Cornish merges most fully into the literature of medieval Europe.[40]

The three plays performed over three days cover the beginning of the world, Christ's passion and his resurrection, that is, the major narratives which formed the core beliefs of Christian Europe. At the time the plays were performed late in the fourteenth century, Cornwall was and felt itself to be an integral part of Christendom, not a provincial English backwater. Despite the profound seriousness of the narrative, often expressed in moving verse, the quality of the writing is lively and demotic, as in:

> "you whip him like a sissy, better at blowing big farts than delivering big blows! But with my lash, whistle-wham! I'll face you down Jesus, oh you rascal! And make you a present of a wicked hiding!"[41]

The language of the play is inclusive, and speaks to the whole community, reinforcing its shared beliefs, the beliefs which brought

---

Performance, Bristol: Redcliffe.

39 See Grigg, E. (2008). "The Medieval Cornish Bible: More Evidence". In Payton, P. (ed), (2008*). Cornish Studies* 16.

40 Murdoch, *op. cit.*, p. 41.

41 In Markham Harris's translation. Harris, M. (1909). *The Cornish Ordinalia: A Medieval Dramatic Trilogy*. Washington DC, Caqtholic University of America Press, p. 142.

it together in worship, the beliefs which, at this point in its history, it shared with the rest of Europe.

Nineteenth-century scholars, though their work in editing and publishing the Cornish texts was invaluable, were frequently dismissive of their literary quality. In the introduction to his edition of the *Ordinalia* Edwin Norris wrote:

> There is nothing in these dramas that may not be found in such as have been printed in English, French and Latin, under the designation of mysteries or miracle plays.[42]

But this is not the case. Certainly the *Ordinalia* trilogy is part of a wider European tradition, treats of similar themes and has many characteristics in common with it, as one would expect, but as Brian Murdoch makes clear, it does have distinctive qualities of its own.[43] Firstly it is of course written in Cornish, though it contains loan words from French, Latin and English, most memorably the beautiful song of the Three Maries. Secondly, all the Cornish plays were performed in an open-air amphitheatre such as the one at St Just, and surviving manuscripts contain sketches to guide production, which clearly indicate that action took place at different levels on the mound (which was often an ancient hill fort adapted for the purpose), and that different characters occupied different positions around the stage. The staging plan allowed emphasis to be placed on themes of doctrinal and dramatic importance, while guaranteeing that all the audience was involved, an accessible dramaturgy which anticipated the twentieth-century "theatre in the round".[44]

Thirdly, the plays were carefully located in the Penryn area, with most of the place-names mentioned falling within a ten-mile radius of Glasney College, strengthening the argument that they were written by one of the canons resident there. The place-names usually designate land grants in return for services rendered, as in:

---

42 Norris, E. (1859). *The Ancient Cornish Drama*. Oxford, Oxford University Press.
43 Murdoch, *op. cit.*, p. 62.
44 Bakere, J. (1980). *The Cornish Ordinalia: A Critical Study*. Cardiff, University of Wales Press, pp. 151-169.

messyger rag the seruys
the rewardye my a ra
carn suyow ha trehembys
chathur annethe thy's gura (2309-12)

Messenger, for thy service
I will reward thee;
Carnsew and Trehembys
Make of them a charter for thyself[45]

No doubt some of the place-names contain topical references or jokes which are lost to us but would have had meaning for the contemporary audience. An interesting example is the Bishop's gift to the torturers in the play:

my a rea
thyugh an dremma
hag ol chennary an clos (2770-72)

I will give
To you these places,
And all Chennary of the Close.[46]

A local audience would have no doubts whatsoever about the character of a bishop who gave their proud borough, over which we have no jurisdiction at all, to such people as Maximilla's murderers (in the play)

Especially perhaps if the bishop was an Englishman in distant Exeter.

Though not entirely unique to Cornwall the *Ordinalia*'s dramatization of the legend of the Holy Rood does distinguish it from the major English play cycles, such as those of York and Chester. The

45 Norris, *op. cit.*, p. 174-75.
46 *Ibid.*, p. 41. Clarified by Nance's emendation of Norris's mistranslation, to be found in Nance's version of the *Ordinalia* in typescript at The Royal Institution of Cornwall.

legend traces the cross upon which Christ was crucified (the Holy Rood) from Adam, who is given the twigs from which it later grows, to Christ. The story of this fateful wood is traced through Moses, David, Solomon and so on. Other stories include a visit by Seth to Paradise where he receives the seeds from which the tree is grown which later provides the wood for the cross.[47] The Cornish dramatist probably used an anonymous thirteenth century Latin version of the story.

In the first of the Cornish plays, the *Origo Mundi*, God promises the "Oil of Mercy" to Adam and Eve as they are expelled from the Garden, as Adam pleads for his sentence to be mitigated:

> A das dev y'th wolowys
> grannt the'th whythres me a'd peys
> nep peyth a oel a vercy (325-71)

> O Father, God, in they light,
> Grant to thy workmanship, I pray thee,
> Some of the oil of mercy.[48]

God then promises Adam that he will be given the Oil of Mercy *yn dyweth a'n bys*, 'in the end of the world'. Later as Adam lies on his deathbed, his son Seth is sent to Paradise to request the Oil of Mercy. Seth is shown a vision of the Christ child in the withered branches of the Tree of Knowledge, cursed by Adam's sin, and is told:

> ef yv an oyl a versy
> a fue the'th tas dythywys
> dre y vernans yredy
> ol an bys a fyth sylwys (815-18)

> He is the oil of mercy,
> Which was promised to thy father;

47 Murdoch, *op. cit.* See also Quinn, E. C. (1962). *The Quest of Seth.* Chicago, University of Chicago Press. And Halliday, G. E. (1955). *The Legend of the Rood.* London, Duckworth.
48 Norris, *op. cit.*, pp. 24-25.

Through his death, clearly,
All the world will be saved.[49]

The angel gives Seth three seeds and he returns home. When Adam dies Seth plants the seeds under his tongue and they grow into rods which play different roles in Old Testament history, until they are eventually incorporated into Solomon's temple, and subsequently become a bridge over the brook of Cedron, and from here the torturers remove them to make the cross of Christ. In this series of startling and paradoxical images, the healing oil of mercy is identified with the Christ child, and the crucifixion, through which Christ's sacrifice becomes possible. The first man is saved from his sin, just as we, the audience, are saved by the death and resurrection of Christ, the second Adam.

The theme of the trilogy then is the universal story of Christ's death and resurrection, which would have been recognized all over fourteenth-century Europe. But this "big narrative" is framed in a distinctively Cornish way, staged in the heart of the community in a place which recalls its past, and in a language which celebrated its identity and continuity. Even the place-names cited in the text identify the Palestine within which the story is set with the Cornish landscape well-known to the audience. The unique setting of the *plen an gwary* must have involved the audience in a direct and powerful way.[50] The boundaries to which we are accustomed in the modern theatre were deliberately blurred. We must remember too that there were once eighty to ninety playing places in west Cornwall, and even if they were also used for other purposes, most of the Cornish-speaking population must have had access to one.[51] Parish records also suggest that many plays were performed which were subsequently lost. The Blanchminster Charity Records from Stratton record a play of Robyn Hoode, which was also played at St Columb Major, and this was clearly a popular secular piece. The St Breock churchwardens accounts record payments for a play about Suzanna

---

49 *Ibid.*, pp. 62-63.
50 Ray Edwards' story "An Asyn" captures the atmosphere. Edwards, R. (1994). *An Asyn.* Kesva an Taves Kernewek.
51 Bakere, *op. cit.*, pp. 16-18.

an unusual and interesting choice of biblical subject, virtually unknown elsewhere in Britain.[52]

As we have seen, the performance of the *Ordinalia*, though no account of an actual performance survives, must have served to evoke the culture and identity of its audience. But perhaps the plays, though their primary focus is salvation history, also speak to Cornwall's contemporary situation; the Egyptian captivity of the children of Israel, for instance, which is punished by a great plague.

> an dour ha'n eys yv posnys
> maythens mur a tus dyswreys
>   ha bestes certan y'th wlas
> nynsyw aga dev pleysys
> genes gy pan os punsys
>   ty ha'th pobel mar calas (1559-64)

> The water and the corn are poisoned,
> So that many of the men are destroyed,
>   And beasts, certainly in thy land.
> Their God is not pleased
> With thee, since thou art punished,
>   Thou and thy people so severely.[53]

This could recall Britain's terrible experience with the Black Death, which reached Cornwall in 1348, causing the evacuation of Truro.[54]

The play also contains the famous story of David's desire for Bathsheba, the wife of Uriah the Hittite. In order to possess her, David sends Uriah on a hopeless military mission on which he is killed. God sends the angel Gabriel to rebuke the king:

> gortheb thy'm ty myghtern bras
> den an geffe cans dauas

---

52 *Ibid.*, p. 19. The dramatic story of Suzanna, rescued from accusations of infidelity by the prophet Daniel, is considered apocryphal by the Protestant churches. Robin Hood plays also had an emancipatory theme.

53 Norris, *op. cit.*, pp. 118-119.

54 Harris, *op. cit.*, p. 25.

ha'y kentrevek saw onan
mar a's ladtre theworto
pan pyn a gotho thotho
    lauar en guyr thy'm certan (2229-34)

    Answer me, thou mighty king:
    A man may possess a hundred sheep,
      And his neighbour only one;
    If he steal it from him,
    What punishment is due to him?
      Tell me the truth, certainly.[55]

This sense of injustice and oppression is of course present in the scriptural account from which the episode is taken, but it may have had a particular resonance in a Cornwall which, a hundred years later, was to rise in rebellion provoked by taxes that were perceived as unjust.[56] The King David scenes, a few verses later, are located in Cornwall, which may be significant.[57]

The play of Christ's passion contains a reference to Peter's "pair of swords". Markham Harris comments that:

by the medieval Cornishman even mildly sensitive to the ideological climate of his age, the two swords of this passage might well be interpreted as symbols of the twin powers, spiritual and temporal, of church and state.[58]

These powers later clashed when Cornwall's religious institutions, including Glasney College where this play was composed, were suppressed in Tudor times. Glasney was dedicated to Thomas a Becket who gave his life to preserve the independence of the church from the monarchy in 1170. That the hope of Cornish freedom associated with the return of King Arthur had survived into the time of the *Ordinalia* is shown by an early fifteenth-century poem in the "Red Book of Bath":

55 Norris, *op. cit.*, p. 168.
56 See Fletcher, A. (1968). *Tudor Rebellions.* London, Longmans, pp. 14-16.
57 Norris, *op. cit.*, pp. 174-175.
58 Harris, *op. cit.*, p. 259.

> But for he scaped that batell y-wys
> Bretons once Cornysh sayeth thus
> That he levyth yet, pards
> And shall come and be a king age.[59]

The idea of resistance to foreign oppression is an undercurrent in the play, and this also functions at a cultural level. In the *Passio Domini* play two scholars are summoned into the presence of King Herod to debate Christ's claim to be both God and man. One of the doctors puts the case for his dual nature, after the "second doctor" denies it:

> me a bref bos gow henna
> rak dev ha den yv dev dra
>   pur contraryus yn kende
> dev yv spirys hep body
>   bos an thew-ma na alse (1730-34)

> I will prove that to be a falsehood
> For God and man are two things
>   Very contradictory in nature:
> God is a spirit without body,
> Man is a body with limbs;
>   He could not be both these.

> y gorthyby me a wra
> ef a alse bos yn ta
>   hanter den ha hanter dev
> den yv hanter morvoron
> benen a'n pen the'n colon
>   yn della yw an ihesu (1739-44)

> I will answer him;
> He might be well

---

59 Quoted in Ralegh Radford (1968). "Glastonbury Abbey." In Ashe, Alcock *et al* (1968). *The Quest for Arthur's Britain*. St Albans, Granta.

Half man and half God
Human is half the mermaid,
Woman from the head to the heart;
So is the Jesus.[60]

This image is particularly startling given the misogyny of the time, and captures brilliantly the dual nature of Christ in a characteristically Cornish way. The central theme of the play is thus identified with a figure which was and remains central to the folklore traditions of west Cornwall, an important component of the collective memory in the oral tradition. Henry Jenner wondered if this metaphor explained the presence of mermaids carved on the bench-ends of Cornish churches, including the one at Senara's church at Zennor, at that time the property of Glasney college, about seven miles from the *plen an gwary* at St Just. Mermaids form a distinct category in Robert Hunt's *Romances of the Mythic Ages* and he associated their stories particularly with Morva, between the parishes of St Just and Zennor.[61] Later in the scene we find a reference to "Tryger", one of only three Cornish place names in the *Passio*:

alemma bys yn tryger
war ow fay lacka mester
ny alsen y thyerbyn. (2274-76)

From this place to Treguer,
On my faith, a worse master
I should not be able to meet him.[62]

If "Treguer" means 'Trigg hundred' then the metaphor is an expansive one, meaning "from here to Cornwall's eastern border". The parishes of Trigg are named after the daughters of Brychan "a family of Irish saints which arrived in Cornwall in King Arthur's time".[63] The *Passio* also features Joseph of Arimathea who claims the

60 Norris, *op. cit.*, pp. 360-61.
61 Hunt, *op. cit.*, p. 148.
62 Norris, *op. cit.*, p. 404.
63 See Morris, J. (1973). *The Age of Arthur: A History of the British Isles from 350-650.* London, Weidenfeld and Nicolson, p. 130.

body of Christ for burial, and is present on stage as the play closes. This is of course a part of the account of Christ's death given in the Gospels, and it is also one of the most moving episodes in the play:

>marsyw marow ihesu ker
>neffre theweth vyth ov cher
>lyes torn da yn bys-ma
>re wruk the vohosugyon
>sawye pup eghen clefyon
>a vewhe yn bewnans da (3105-10)

>If dear Jesus is dead,
>Ever ended is my cheer;
>Many good turns in this world
>He hath done to the poor;
>He cured all sorts of sick persons
>Who live in good life.[64]

For the original audiences this episode may also have recalled the folk belief that Joseph of Arimathea had visited Scilly and Cornwall to buy tin, bringing the boy Jesus with him: traditions of this visit survived into modern times at Marazion and Ding Dong in Penrith, St Day, Falmouth and St Just in Roseland.[65] This must also have helped the audience to identify with the play, an effective dramatic strategy which seems to have been followed consistsently, in terms of both content and staging. Although the *Ordinalia*'s main concern is to tell the story of Christ's death and resurrection, it skilfully presents these events in two contexts, the scriptural and the Cornish, simultaneously. This alone defines it as a complex work of dramatic art. It affirms Cornwall's place in the wider community of Christian nations, bound together by the Church which England was about to leave, just as, like the storytelling sessions of later times but in a much more intense way, it celebrates the Cornish identity by invoking its past and present. Though the plays themselves faced a

64 Morris, *op. cit.*, p. 468.
65 See Lewis, Rev. M. A. (no date). *Christ in Cornwall*. Falmouth, J. H. Lake & Co.

bleak future as religious cycles were suppressed in the sixteenth century.

Chapter 2

The Mirror of the Past

The Cornish Passion Poem

The Cornish Passion poem, *Pascon agan Arluth* is the earliest complete Cornish text to have survived.[66] It consists of 259 stanzas describing Christ's Passion and death, and is based mainly on the Gospel narrative. It was the first middle Cornish text to be published, in 1826, by Davies Gilbert, and though its provenance is unknown it seems to be linked to Glasney College, since the *Ordinalia*, known to be from Glasney, borrows some lines from it. Both works focus on what Murdoch calls "the divine economy", Christ's sacrifice to redeem the human race from sin. Of course the poem's intent is devotional and didactic, not public and communal: reading a poem is very different from watching a play.[67]

The poem describes Christ's resistance to temptation in the wilderness before moving on to cover his healing ministry and the hostility of the Jewish establishment, leading up to the betrayal of Judas and the events leading up to the Passion itself.[68] Some motifs anticipate the *Ordinalia*, notably the legend of the smith who refused to make nails for the crucifixion, whose hands miraculously take on a leprous appearance.[69] The narrative also recounts the taking of Christ's body by Joseph, and concludes with a prayer "which is linguistically impressive, with a complexity of rhyme and echoes, and some anaphora which links with the crucifixion and the Good Thief but makes clear, and this is of great importance, the significance of the narrative for the listener".[70] Woodhouse translates:

---

66 Murdoch, *op. cit.*, pp. 19-40.
67 Though it may of course have been read aloud.
68 Gilbert, D. (1826). *Mount Calvary*. London, Nichols.
69. Murdoch, *op. cit.*, p. 23.
70 Murdoch, *op. cit.*, p. 23.

As Christ arose from his tomb, then on the third day, so shall
we all rise on Judgement Day, evil and good also, the work
of the good man shall grow, he shall be rich then, the wicked
man on that day, woe to him, he shall be on Christ's left
hand.[71]

The poem highlights the sorrow of a people which has lost its
homeland because of the sin of Adam:

> An dus vas a ʒeserya
> ʒeʒe gulas nef o kyllys
> gans aga garm hag olua
> ihesus crist a ve mevijs (25-28)

> The good folk were desiring
> for themselves the Heaven that was lost.
> by their outcry and lamentation,
> Jesus Christ was moved.[72]

The poem's treatment of the trial scene hinges on Jesus' supposed
challenge to Roman authority:

> ytho mygtern ote se yn meth pylat an erna
> gwyr re gwesys yredy yn meth crist mygtern oma (817-20)

> "Then, art thou a king?" said Pilate then.
> "Thou hast spoken truth indeed" said Christ. "A king I am."[73]

This incident is of course scriptural, but it may have had a
subversive resonance for a people which still remembered its own
lost Christian king and awaited his return. The trial scene is
illustrated by a line drawing, one of ten "rude pictures" which
illustrate the manuscript, which may underline its importance.

---

71 Woodhouse, H. (2002). *The Cornish Passion Poem in Facsimile*. Gorseth Kernow,
    p. 97.
72 Woodhouse, *op. cit.*, p. 15.
73 Woodhouse, *op. cit.*, p. 49.

Davies Gilbert, the poem's first editor, in words that recall Edwin Norris's comments in his edition of the *Ordinalia*, dismisses it thus:

> No-one more sincerely rejoices than does the Editor of this ancient mystery, that the Cornish dialect of the Celtic or Gaelic (sic) language has ceased altogether from being used by the inhabitants of Cornwall; whatever may have been its degree of intrinsic excellence: experience amply demonstrating that no infliction on a province is equally severe or irremediable as the separation by distinct speech from a great and enlightened nation of which it forms a part, a separation closing against it most of the avenues to knowledge, and wholly intercepting that course of rapid improvement which eminently distinguishes the present age from all other periods in the history of man.[74]

One can only wonder why he bothered to edit the poem at all. This unpleasant mixture of smugness and racism was not uncommon among British scholars toward the Cornish language and its literature, and seems to conceal an underlying insecurity as the century moved on and Victorian confidence and optimism gave way to anxiety and doubt, even in the "great and enlightened nation", as the England of Jane Austen was transformed into the England of *Our Mutual Friend* and *Bleak House*.

The *Pascon agan Arluth*, though occasionally moving, is not a great work of art though, nor is it an enactment of shared memory like the *Ordinalia*. It is however an important source for the later plays, and it affirmed Cornwall's place as a distinct nation in the wider European community. In this sense the story of the Passion in Cornish moved from written text to communal drama. In the nineteenth century Hunt's stories moved in the opposite direction, from shared event to printed text. Each of these transitions involves a change of audience, and changes of style, vocabulary and interpretation.

---

74 Gilbert, *op. cit.*, p. vii.

The Life of Meriasek

This work is a two-day dramatic cycle in Middle Cornish of around 4500 lines of rhymed verse, and was unique in that it dealt with a non-biblical saint.[75] Meriasek lived in the fifth or sixth century, and seems to have been born in Wales, though his cult was apparently confined to Cornwall and Brittany, in both of which countries he was active. It is thought that the play was written around the year 1504, shortly after the Cornish insurrection of 1497, led by Flamank and An Gof, who marched a Cornish army to Blackheath, where they were defeated.[76] The rising was provoked by excessive taxation and what Polydore Vergil described as "the cruelty and malice of counsellors... the authors of this great oppression".[77] Cornwall obviously had long-standing grievances and was ripe for rebellion. An Gof and Flamank were hanged, drawn and quartered, but their names are still honoured in Cornwall. The other rebels were treated with a leniency which may seem surprising at first sight, but is explained by Polydore Vergil:

> the king would have ordered that the dismembered corpses of Thomas Flammock (sic) and Michael Joseph (An Gof) should be displayed in various places throughout Cornwall, in order that the penalties of treason might be widely known and seen: but when he heard that those who had stayed at home were not cowed by the catastrophe that had befallen their fellows, but were still keen to begin a rebellion if they were roused in any way, Henry changed his mind for fear he might embarrass himself with ever greater burdens at a time when he considered it enough to end civil strife.[78]

It was against this troubled background that the "Life of Meriasek" was written and staged. As Alan Kent's reading of the play shows, the Cornish response was cultural as well as political and military. Philip Payton had already argued that the play was "a subversive

---

75 Until the manuscript of *Bewnans Ke* was discovered in 2000.
76 At least the play was copied in 1504, perhaps for performance, by Radulphus Ton.
77 Payton, P. (2004). *Cornwall: A History*. Fowey, Cornwall Editions, pp. 1007-10.
78 *Ibid.*, pp. 110-11.

document, a vehicle for Cornish identity..."[79] Payton identified Teudar, the tyrant in the play, as "an outsider imposing his power".

The first scene begins in Brittany, where Meriasek grew up, describing his education and his father's attempt to force him into a dynastic marriage, which he resists, saying "my wish is to be a knight of God". He is ordained as a priest and goes to Cornwall, where he settles in Camborne where he performs a number of miracles before encountering Teudar, a local pagan tyrant, whom he attempts to convert to Christianity, without success: Teudar here appears to be identical with the Teudar who features in "The Life of St Kea". He also appears in the "lives" of a number of fifth century saints, including Fingar, Petroc and Breaca, invariably as a tyrannical pagan king attempting to hinder the propagation of the Christian faith. Though the saints' lives were written much later, as were the plays, this may represent a traditional memory of pagan opposition in the age of the saints: it may also be that the form of the name, "Teudar" is an allusion to the Tudor dynasty which was deeply unpopular in Cornwall following the crushing of the rebellion in 1497 and perhaps before.

After a rather sophisticated theological argument Meriasek dedicates a chapel at Camborne to Mary the mother of Christ, then flies to Britanny and builds another chapel. The next part of the play concerns the life of Saint Sylvester, and features the emperor Constantine whose leprosy is healed after he refuses to sacrifice children to seek a cure.

In the second part of the "Life of Meriasek" the Duke of Cornwall, the rightful ruler, overthrows the evil Teudar, despite his demonic supporters. The first day is concluded, and the audience is invited to attend on the following day to see the concluding part of the play:

> Evugh oll gans an guary
> ny a vyn agis pesy
> a luen golon
> wy agis beth gor ha gruek

79 Payton, P. "A Concealed Envy against the English: A Note on the Aftermath of the 1497 Rebellions in Cornwall". In Payton, P. (1992). *Cornish Studies 1*, pp. 4-13.

banneth crist ha meryasek
banneth maria cambron
pybugh menstrels colonnek
may hyllyn donsia dyson (2505-12)

Drink ye all with the play
we will beseech you
with a full heart.
Ye shall have, man and woman,
The blessing of Christ and Meriasek
  The blessing of Mary of Camborne.
Pipe ye, hearty minstrels,
  That we may be able to dance forthwith.[80]

In the Interlude which begins the second day Constantine appears announcing the conversion of Rome to Christianity, and the authority of the Church over the secular power: "The Emperor's crown is mine" (I 2515) In the third part of the Meriasek play the blind Earl Globus goes in search of Meriasek to ask him to restore his sight. The saint cures him, and also people suffering from deafness and demonic possession. The Earl of Vannes tries to make Meriasek a bishop, but he refuses and goes on to perform more miracles, incuding the cure of a naked sick man who describes his plight in moving verses indentifying himself with the suffering Christ:

A rag ou an golyov
a thuk crist cleth ha dyov
  the vap den rag saluasconn
ov corff vy yv antythy
  numcar neb lues map bron

Menogh gans yrgh ha clehy
me re vue in mes dre nos
rewys an doyr pur defry
ov golyov luen a plos
  . prest ov sclaldya (3049-59)

---

80. Stokes, W. (1872). *Beunans Meriasek*. London, Trübner and Co, pp. 144-45.

O for all the wounds
Which Christ bore, left and right,
For salvation to the son of man!
My body is powerless,
Rotten, stricken are my veins
Not any son of a breast loves me.

Often with hail and ice
I have been out through night,
The ground frozen right earnestly.
My wounds full of filth
Always inflaming.[81]

This episode is followed by the separate play called "The woman's son", in which a young man goes to the court of "King Massen" to "learn to be manly".[82] This name is interesting and may preserve a memory of "Macsen Wledig", as he was known in Welsh (in the story "The Dream of Macsen Wledig" in the *Mabinogion* for instance).[83] He was a Roman Emporer in the fourth century CE whose real name was Maximus Clemens, and he was a hero to the British because he helped them to overthrow the rule of Gratian in 383.[84] In this entertaining play a statesmanlike King Masson confronts a tyrant ("Sir Tyrant go on your way/Never will there come a day/when you are born to kingship") and the "woman's son" is released from prison by the intercession of the Blessed Virgin Mary, emphasizing the theme of emancipation from unjust authority. Arguments about legitimacy are found everywhere in Cornish drama—witness the fascinating debate about Christ's kingship in the *Ordinalia*'s trial scene. If the Cornish questioned the legitimacy of English rule, and their growing incorporation into "a great and enlightened nation" this could only be done in code: that this was consciously intended by the dramatist or directly apprehended by the audience is unclear, but that it directly addressed their concerns at this precise historical

81 Ibid., pp. 176-77.
82 Whitley Stokes glosses 'Massen' as 'Maximus'.
83 See Jones, G. and Jones, T. (1949). *The Mabinogion*. London, Dent and Sons, pp. 79-88.
84 McKillop, *op. cit.*, p. 49.

ment cannot be doubted. Texts, like people often say more than
they mean.

In the fourth part of the play, Meriasek returns, performs another
miracle (emphasizing his own legitimacy as a servant of God), and
is comforted by the Angel Gabriel. The play then concludes the "Life
of Sylvester", in which the saint overcomes a dragon and wins more
converts to Christ.

> Cans den lethys war ov feth
> nav re vue sur in vn geth
>> prest gensy hy
> mar qureth y ouercummya
> the crist ny a vyn treyla
>> var off ny yllyth defry (4009-14)

> A hundred men slain, on my faith
> Now were surely in one day
>> By her. [i.e., the dragon]
> If thou canst overcome her
> To Christ we will turn.
>> I am aware that thou wilt not be able really.[85]

Here, as elsewhere miracles serve as a sign of legitimacy.

The play concludes with the death of Meriasek, and a final
valediction from the Earl of Vannes:

> Dywhy banneth meryasek
> ha maria cambron wek
>> banneth an abesteleth
> evugh oll gans an guary
> ny a vyn agis pesy
>> kyns moys an plaeth (4557-62)

> To you the blessing of Meriasek,
> And of sweet Mary of Camborne,
>> The blessing of the apostles!

---

85 Stokes, *op. cit.*, pp. 232-33.

25

Drink ye all with the play
We will beseech you
Before going from the place.[86]

Meriasek lived perhaps a thousand years before "the Camborne play" was written, and the strength of the tradition illustrates important themes in the transmission of Cornish culture. Firstly of course the significance of the language itself, and of the communal setting in which the play is enacted, reinforced by the closing words of the play. Secondly the strength of the Meriasek tradition itself, and the traditions of all the other saints whose names still dot the Cornish countryside. No doubt the stories of Meriasek had been embellished over the years, and much material must have been lost, but the essential picture of the saint of healer, founder and preacher emerges with remarkable clarity. This must have been particularly important at a time when the English ecclesiastical authorities were attempting to integrate the Cornish Church by rededicating parish churches bearing the names of Cornish saints. Thirdly, though it is not central to the play's purpose which is primarily to impart religious teaching, there is an interesting subtext dealing with authority and power, its obligations and limitations. This late efflorescence of Cornish literature and language produced a sophisticated work of art carrying a powerful message to its audience, a mirror to reflect its own threatened identity.

The Life of St Kea
The continuing vitality of traditional storytelling is also revealed in the *Bewnans Ke* trilogy. Like *Beunans Meriasek* it testifies to the continuity of Cornish faith and culture over a millennium, from the age of saints to the Renaissance, a continuity which was to be shattered by the Reformation and the imposition of the English Prayer Book, which had dire consequences for Cornwall.

The text of *Bewnans Ke* was discovered among the papers of Professor J. E. Caerwyn Williams on his death, and he left no record of its provenance. Five folios are missing at the beginning and end and two further folios between folios eight and nine. What remains

86 *Ibid.*, pp. 264-65.

has been damaged by mice at some stage, and as with so many other Cornish stories what remains seems to have survived by chance, as wreckage washed up by the sea of history, fragments from a lost land.

The cult of St Kea seems always to have been limited to the area surrounding old Kea church in Cornwall and to Britanny.[87] Though a later life of the saint by Albert Le Grand does exist, his origins and even his name are still subject to scholarly debate. What is clear is that, like many Celtic saints of the time, he travelled extensively around the Celtic seaboard. As the play begins, in the form in which we have it, St Ke mounts a stone and floats across the sea to Cornwall (this was a frequent motif: St Piran made the crossing from Ireland on a stone; saints David, Brynach and Stinan made similar journeys, and Saint Ia arrived from Ireland floating on a leaf).

Ke is taken to see King Teudar at Goodron Castle where he is accused of stealing the king's stags. Ke tries to convert the king to Christianity but is thrown into prison, where he finds comfort in prayer. The gaolers report that he is surrounded by a heavenly light and sweet odours. Teudar, impressed, has Ke released, and tries unsuccessfully to persuade him to renounce Christianity. Ke asks the king for a plot of land in "Rosewa" where he can live in peace. Teudar agrees on condition that Ke does not abuse his pagan gods, and at this point there is a gap in the manuscript. When the text resumes we learn that Ke has been tortured, and this has merely caused him to praise God all the more: this enrages Teudar, who dismissed his torturers. This part of the text is particularly fragmented, and we are reminded again of the fragility of tradition.[88]

Ke journeys on to Rosewa and prays for water. A well miraculously springs up, and he uses the water to heal a leper, who in his gratitude gives the well and the surrounding land to Ke, who goes on to Rosewa where stags arrive and allow themselves to be yoked to the plough.[89] Teudar sends a messenger to make peace,

---

87 For this and what follows, see the Introduction to Thomas, G. and Williams, N. (2007). *The Life of St Kea: A Critical Edition*. Exeter, University of Exeter Press.

88 Ibid., pp. 68-9.

89 In pagan Britain stags were magical beasts, and this incident may originally have signified the triumph of Christianity: the Christianized stag became a guide to Heaven. See MacKillop, *op. cit.*, p. 46. Similarly miraculous cures demonstrated the superior power of Christian magic. St Petroc was also associated

but Ke says he will never befriend a pagan king. Nonetheless Teudar regrets what he has done and desires reconciliation: he offers Ke as much land as he can enclose during the time the king takes a bath, and with the help of Oubra, a wise woman he tricks Teudar and takes his best land:

> Me a wor gwyer hag a'n crys
> bos ke thotha drehevys,
>   theworth Kewnans an Velyn
>   bys in Tremustel Penpol,
>   A'n mor the gela cowal. (1195-99)

> I know truly and believe it
> That he has built a hedge
> From Kewnans an Velyn
> To Tremustel by Penpol
> Wholly from one sea to the other.[90]

This verse contains a pun on the saint's name *Ke* and *ke*, the low, banked Cornish hedge. The saint is thus identified with the landscape, just as he is credited with shaping it, as the founder of the Christian community, creator of wells and churches. Finally Teudar curses his god, and the text breaks off, to resume at the point when Arthur's conflict with Rome begins as the king addresses his assembled allies, and the scene then moves to the court of the Emperor Lucius Hiberius, who sends messengers to Britain demanding the customary tribute. When it was re-staged in the sixteenth century, the audience surely recalled the unjust levy which led to their own rising. More leaves are missing, and when the play resumes Arthur is preparing for battle and reiterating his refusal to pay the tribute:

> Lavar the'th arluth, cosyn:
>   me re leverys teb flows,
>   rag an trubut a wovyn
>   na goyth nahen war nebas ous

---

with stags.
90 Thomas and Williams, *op. cit.*, pp. 124-25.

the'n stat a Rome,
   mars e ben ef dybbynys.
   Mar goyth pan ew govynnys
   by the dredful day of dom! (2112-20)

Tell your lord, my friend:
I have said without trifling,
as for the tribute he demands,
there does not fall for some time now
to the state of Rome,
anything other than his decapitated head.
Since it is insolently demanded,
I shall send it thither indeed,
by the dreadful day of doom![91]

This must have brought the house down. The messengers then return to Rome and Lucius and his allies depart for Gaul to fight Arthur. In the next scene Arthur says goodbye to his wife Guinevere and leaves her, and Britain, in the hands of his nephew Modred. In Arthur's absence Modred seduces Guinevere and forces the bishop to crown him king, in yet another example of illegitimate rule: when Arthur hears of this he returns to Britain. In the meantime Modred has sent Chellery Duke of the Saxons to recruit pagan mercenaries in German in return for grants of land in Kent and the north. Arthur and Modred's armies meet, and several of Arthur's friends are killed, though he is eventually victorious. The queen hears this news, and the play ends abruptly, in the absence of the last five leaves.

The fragmentary nature of the text makes the play difficult to interpret. Parallels with the Breton life of the saint suggest that a missing scene showed the reconciliation of Ke and Teudar, the cure of the king's mental distress and his conversion to Christianity followed by Ke's departure for Britanny. A major problem with the play is the relationship between the story of Ke and the Arthurian material. In the "Life" Ke and others are sent to mediate between Arthur and Modred because of the threat to Christianity posed by Chellery and the Saxons. The motif of saintly intervention to resolve

---

91 *Ibid.*, pp. 212-13.

secular disputes is common in Celtic hagiography—St Ronan for instance tries to reconcile the warring parties at Magh Rath in Ireland.[92]

Though the opening scenes are missing, the play clearly illustrates the interconnectedness of the Celtic world in the age of the saints. Like Ke Saint Piran reached Cornwall by floating from Ireland on a millstone. The Welsh saint Brychan came to Cornwall with his twenty-four sons and twenty-five daughters, all of them saints.[93] Again the themes of faith, redemption and healing link Cornwall with the wider European culture, and the memory of the saint as healer, founder and preacher lives still. The Arthurian scenes, though probably influenced by European romance, are even more striking testimony to the power of memory to define and reflect cultural identity. They represent the only surviving Arthurian narrative in Cornish, although Cornwall's special links with the legendary king have long been recognized, and are attested in folklore,[94] for instance. Despite continuing scholarly debate over Arthur's identity and sphere of operations, the Cornish dramatist has no doubt where Arthur belongs. When he first appears he is:

> ow arluth, flowran an bys,
> a Gyllywyk.
> Arthur ew henna heb flows (1285-87)

> my lord, the flower of the world,
> of Kellywyk.
> That is Arthur without any nonsense.[95]

"Kellywyk" or Kelliwic is probably a hillfort at Egloshayle near Padstow. Later in the play he is described as *Arthur Cornow* 'Arthur the Cornishman', *gwelha gour / a ve bythqueth a Gurnow*, 'the best man

92 See O'Donovan, J. (1995 reprint). *The Banquet of Dun Na Gedh and The Battle of Magh Rath*. Felinfach, Llanerch.
93 Halliday, F. E. (1959). *A History of Cornwall*. London, Duckworth, p. 87.
94 See Hunt *op. cit.* under 'Romances of Arthur', pp. 303-13.
95 Thomas and Williams, *op. cit.*, p. 132-33.

who ever came from Cornwall', and *Arthor Gornow, myghtern eresh,* 'Arthur the Cornishman, a truculent king.'[96]

On the other hand this is no Dark Age chieftain, fighting a desperate rearguard action against the invading Saxons, but a mighty king to whom other kings pay tribute, the imperial Arthut of medieval romance, capable of defeating Rome itself, although in historical fact he himself represented the vestigial authority of Rome against barbarian usurpation and in the play he represents legitimate authority. There is clearly an element of idealization here, and quite possibly non-Cornish literary influence. The dramatic effect is to set up a tension between the Cornish king and the Roman emperor, which is resolved when Arthur sends Lucius's head to Rome:

> Ow canhas ker, ke thegy
> bys in Rom gans pen Lucy
>   ha por harth the'n senators
>   trybut Bretayn presant a
>   in dyscharg thymmo nefra
>   ha the ol ow successors. (2838-43)

> My dear messenger, go
> to Rome with the head of Lucius
> and very forcefully to the senators
> present it as Britain's tribute
> to discharge my debt forever
> and that of all my successors.[97]

Arthur's role here is to safeguard British/Cornish independence, and the argument is about legitimacy, as it is elsewhere in Cornish drama. This theme though in a different key, surfaces again in the conflict between Arthur and Modred, when Modred takes his uncle's wife and has himself crowned King of Britain

---

96 *Ibid.*, pp. 170, 192, 250.
97 *Ibid.*, pp 282-3.

Triadic Relations

This triadic relationship, in which three characters are bound together in a tragic conflict of loyalty and desire had a particular appeal for Celtic storytellers.[98] Ireland had its stories of Fionn MacCumhaill, Diarmuid and Grainne, of Deirdriu, Naoise and Wales its story of Blodeuwedd, Lleu and Gronw Pebyr, lord, the vengeful Conchsbar, lord of Penllyn; Cornwall its tragedy of Tristan, Eseult and Mark, which became renowned throughout Europe in the Middle Ages.[99] The story of Arthur, Guinevere and Modred, whether it is historically factual or not, falls into this narrative pattern. The core story is that of an ageing king who takes a beautiful young wife (whose own wishes of course are not consulted). She falls in love with a handsome young man and vice versa. The young hero is also bound to the king by ties of loyalty, which were particularly strong in early warbound societies. The king in turn loves his young retainer, and these insoluble tensions inevitably lead to a tragic ending.

On one level the story illustrates a dilemma which could have been terribly real in early, heroic society, a dilemma with potentially destructive and divisive consequences, not just for the individuals concerned. And the conflict between Arthur and Mordred (variously spelt Modred, Medraut, Modres) have drastic results for the people of Britain, of which Cornwall was an important part: Modred's seduction of the queen and the civil war which it caused divided the British resistance to Saxon invasion and led to defeat and occupation.[100] In the play Modred sends to Germany to summon more Saxons to help him fight Arthur, and here the playwright seems to be following Geoffrey of Monmouth's account in his *History of the Kings of Britain*, as he does in describing the war against the Romans. Modred's illegitimate seizure of power was thus a disastrous event

98 See McMahon (2006). *The Princess who Ate People: The Psychology of Celtic Myth.* Wymeswold, Heart of Albion, Chapter 3.

99 A very early triadic story is Plutarch's "The Poisoned Libation: The Love Triangle of Sinatus, Sinorix and the High Priestess Camma". In Koch, J. (ed) (2003). *The Celtic Heroic Age: Literary Sources for Ancient Celtic Europe and Early Ireland and Wales.* Aberystwyth, Celtic Studies Publications, pp. 40-42.

100 See Geoffrey of Monmouth (1966). *The History of the Kings of Britain* (trans Thorpe, L.). Harmondsworth, Penguin.

in the history of the British Celts, a portion of whom eventually became the Cornish people. According to tradition the last battle between the king and his nephew took place at Slaughter Bridge near Camelford, named "Camblan" by Geoffrey.[101] Whether or not this is true, it does constitute evidence of popular belief, especially as a flat stone with a weathered Latin inscription is to be found a few miles upstream, known locally as King Arthur's tomb.[102] In Geoffrey's account Arthur's end is more ambiguous:

> Arthur himself, our renowned king, was mortally wounded, and was carried off to the Isle of Avalon, so that his wounds might be attended to[103]

and this passage has no doubt contributed to the legend that Arthur is not dead but only sleeps, to rule again at the time of his people's greatest need, a belief which survived in Cornwall. Or perhaps Geoffrey reflects such a belief among the people in his own time. At this point it is unclear whether literature describes history or engages creatively with it. Geoffrey claims to have based his work on "a certain very ancient book written in the British language... attractively composed to form a consecutive and orderly narrative", and he also says that the deeds of the British "were handed joyfully down in oral tradition, just as if they had been committed to writing by many peoples who had only their memory to rely on".[104] His own relationship to the oral tradition is unclear. There is no doubt however that the Arthurian section of *Bewnans Ke* is based on Geoffrey's *History* combined with Cornish traditions respecting Arthur.[105]

The Latin "Life of Kea" suggests that the saint did intervene to resolve the conflict, but if this incident was ever part of the Cornish play it is now missing. Dramatically a shift back to the life of St Kea

---

101 *Ibid.*, pp. 260-1.
102 See Westwood, J. (1987). *Albion: A Guide to Legendary Britain*. London, Paladin, pp. 34-5.
103 Geoffrey, *op. cit.*, p. 261.
104 The "British language" was of course the ancestor of Cornish as was the language of the oral tradition. See Geoffrey, op. cit., p. 51.
105 Thomas, G. and Williams, N., *op. cit.*, p. xxx.

seems to be called for after the Arthurian scenes but we will probably never know. The playwright clearly intended to demonstrate how certain places, no doubt well-known to the audience, were acquired by or associated with St Kea. Graham Thomas and Nicholas Williams believe that the play was probably intended to be performed in St Kea parish itself, perhaps on the 3rd of October, the saint's feast day.[106] This would have affirmed the legitimacy of the parish claim to the land, in case of dispute, and this issue of legitimacy is also the main theme uniting the two sections of the play as we have it: who owns the land? Two separate playing places did formerly exist within the parish boundaries.

Parallels have been noted between *Bewnans Ke* and *Beunans Meriasek*. Both saints are also venerated in Brittany, and both are persecuted by a local tyrant called Teudar. These parallels, together with the local placenames, suggest a common link to Glasney College, where the plays were probably written. Both Camborne and Kea parish had strong links with the college.[107] The plays seem to have been written at about the same time, (Thomas and Williams suggest 1453-60),[108] that is, at a time when the legitimate king of England, Henry VI, was imprisoned and Richard of York had himself declared Protector and was reigning in all but name. The issue of political legitimacy was therefore very much in the air, in Cornwall and elsewhere, and what survives of late medieval Cornish drama offers a unique perspective on the theoretical and practical dilemma surrounding the legitimacy of authority in both Cornwall and Britain. A failure to resolve these issues led to the bloodbath which followed Cornwall's "Prayer Book Rebellion" in 1548.

---

106 *Ibid.*, pp xl-xli.
107 *Ibid.*, p. xiiii.
108 *Ibid.*, p. xlvi.

Chapter 3

The Broken Mirror

Reflections

Culture, including film and literature is a mirror in which we may see ourselves, though it is inconvenient and unwise to spend one's entire life in the bathroom. We need mirrors to remind us of who we are. In historical terms it is only comparatively recently that most people have been able to see what they look like. For by far the greater part of human history most people have only been able to see their own image in still water.

Mirrors would seem to have been particularly important to the ancient Celts. The best examples of these objects belong, interestingly enough, to the "western mirror school", which flourished in south-western Britain in the first century CE. The most famous example of this work, the Holcombe mirror, was found in Devon in 1970, within the ancient kingdom of Dummonia of which Cornwall was a part, and it may be seen in the British Museum.[109] The moulding on the handle of this hauntingly beautiful object depicts a fantastic owl, or perhaps cat, both symbolizing wisdom in Celtic and other cultures: perhaps the message is that to see and accept oneself as one really is is to be wise. In retrospect these lovely first century polished bronze mirrors seem to symbolize a community which was at ease with its own reflection, which could look at itself without flinching.

The looking-glass or mirror reminds us of change and continuity. It confronts us with what we are, what we have lost and what we are in process of becoming. It also shows us what others see when they see us: past, present and future come together in one image, an image which testifies to how they value us and so how we value

---

109 Brailsford, J. (1975). *Early Celtic Masterpieces from The British Museum*. London, British Museum Publications.

ourselves. Young people still examine their images anxiously before going out to engage with one another, and whether they like what they see sill depend on whether they come from a family, community and culture which values them and which they themselves can value. This is why the denigration of a culture and community has serious psychological consequences.

Mirrors, however are not our earliest source of information about ourselves. The psychoanalyst Donald Winnicott has suggested that our first and most enduring image of ourselves derives from the baby's reflection of itself which it sees in its mother's face: at a time when we are scarcely aware of our own existence we see love and acceptance in our mother's face, and learn that we are good and worthwhile people. During his time at Paddington Green Hospital Winnicott saw perhaps sixty thousand babies, and he learned to be particularly observant of their relationships with their principal carers, concluding that:

> In the early stages of the emotional development of the human infant a vital part is played by the environment which is in fact not yet separated off from the infant by the infant. Gradually the separating off of the not me from the me takes place, and the pace varies, according to the infant and according to the environment. The major changes take place in the separating out of the mother as an objectively perceived environmental feature.[110]

Later the "mirroring" role extends to father and other family members, and eventually to friends, teachers and one's culture. This is why an attack on a person's culture is also an attack on their sense of identity and an intolerant majority inevitably damages a fragile minority culture and the people who belong to it. In a psychological sense we internalize our mother, and later our father, as "good internal objects", which help sustain our sense of self-worth through life. Melanie Klein, a disciple of Freud, believed that this process is central to sexual and psychosocial development. Our parents are the

110 Quoted in Newman, A. (1995). *Non-Compliance in Winnicott's Words: A Companion to the Writings and Work of D. W. Winnicott.* London, Free Association Books.

most important people we encounter and therefore they form a template for our own identity: this does not mean of course that we necessarily need to be brought up by a heterosexual couple. It is a question of psychological function, not biological genes. But the way in which we are brought up will make us feel either happy or unhappy about ourselves or, more often a mixture of the two. The parental role in reality may be shared by a number of people, and is often taken on by uncles, aunts or grandparents. The fundamental role of the mother though, later to be extended, helps to explain the powerful attachment people feel towards their culture, and the powerful sense of loss they feel when that culture is under attack. Storytelling may be one way of resisting this attack—by holding up a mirror to the self to preserve one's true identity.

Culture and Identity

As time goes on we develop a sense of ourselves as part of a particular community or culture, and this sense of identity is often mediated through acts of collective memory, religious ritual or shared narrative in which we can remember our origins and history, the experiences which have made us what we are. Sometimes of course we reject the values we have inherited, though that is less likely to happen in a traditional society within which choice can be limited. People are designed to live in time, and one function of families and communities is to transmit the living past from one generation to another. When the mirror of the past has been broken, as it has been in Cornwall by the loss of the language, religion and institutions which shaped it, the result is cultural and psychological discontinuity.

Athelstan first broke the Cornish mirror eleven hundred years ago, though he did not go on to fully assimilate Cornwall into south-western England, and ambiguous references to shadowy "kings of the west Welsh" persisted for some time: Athelstan's "accommo-dation" seems to have conceded a degree of Cornish autonomy in practice.[111] Though by then Cornwall itself was but a fragment of a civilization which once embraced western Europe, fragmented again as the Roman empire disintegrated, though Arthur inherited some

---

111 See Deacon, B. (2007). *A Concise History of Cornwall. Cardiff.* University of Wales Press, p. 19.

of its legitimacy and kept its memory alive. But Cornwall, like "Wales" is an English construction: it is the land of the "western foreigners", the "filthy race" of the Anglo-Saxon chronicles. Although the Cornish identity was damaged was remained was illuminated by Christianity, and when the canons of Glasney wrote the *Ordinalia* they created a complex work of art in which the audience could share in the sacred narrative and re-experience themselves. The medieval dramatists wrote to instruct, rather than entertain, but they did so within a specific cultural context. Though they held a total allegiance to the universal church they wrote in Cornish for Cornish people, and there was no conflict between those two allegiances. The Cornish remained uniquely themselves while affirming and strengthening their lives with the rest of Christendom, a link which stretched far beyond the British Isles but which was particularly strong with Brittany and Wales.

The legend of the Oil of Mercy, together with the *Beunans Meriasek* constitutes a particularly strong synthesis between Cornish/Celtic tradition and Christian doctrine: some hope that the European Union will eventually achieve the same synthesis between ethnic diversity and international order, though such hopes are fading. But this balance was not to last in Cornwall. The Reformation and the rise of the centralized nation state, two closely linked historical developments, were to sever the links between smaller nations and the wider culture and leave the peoples of Cornwall and Brittany vulnerable to the territorial ambitions of English and French kings. Tenaciously and tragically the Cornish fought for their past and their future, but with the defeat of Flamank and An Gof at Blackheath, and the savage reprisals which followed the Prayer Book Rebellions, the fate of the Cornish language was sealed. The human cost was huge and the cultural loss was scarcely less. Most people in Britain today neither know not care about these events:

> The suppression of Glasney College had robbed the language of both scholarship and status. The imposition of the Book of Common Prayer meant that English was now heard in every Cornish church. The miracle plays, as vehicles of popular culture in the Cornish language, were

either suppressed as subversive or allowed to fossilise as half-understood relics from earlier times.[112]

But a sense of difference remained to the "strange and unquenchable race": it erupted again at the time of the English Civil War and it created a distinctive body of folklore that was rooted in the land and celebrated in shared acts of memory for generations to come.[113]

Folklore

The nineteenth and early twentieth centuries, the age of the pioneering folklorists, led into the Celtic language revivals. This was the period of the great story collections of Luzel in Brittany, Campbell in the Scottish Highlands, and Lady Gregory in Ireland. To this pan-Celtic (and pan-European) literature Cornwall made a distinguished contribution in the shape of Bottrell's *Traditions and Hearthside Stories of West Cornwall* and Robert Hunt's magnificent *Popular Romances of the West of England*. The oral tradition recorded in these works is all but dead: at the time when the collections were made it was already in serious decline, and was remembered chiefly by elderly working people.

These much-loved stories were produced by and for the communities which shared them, in Cornish *an werin*, the common people. Though for the Cornish drolltellers, the Irish shanachies and their counterparts in other Celtic countries, storytelling was a prized gift, the idea of individual authorship, the middle-class ownership of story, was of course unknown. Like medieval cathedrals the tales were the work not of talented specialists who stood above and apart from their communities, but the result of a collective act of creativity by the community itself. They were collected at a time when the Celtic languages themselves had died or were dying, and it is significant that, while many Cornish stories (particularly Cherry of Zennor, Tregeagle and the giant tales) have a highly imaginative, "Celtic" feel to them, the traditional world view is more strongly

---

112 Payton, P. (2004). *Cornwall: A History*. Fowey Cornwall Editions, p. 155.
113 See Stoyle, M. (2005). *Soldiers and Strangers: An Ethnic History of the English Civil War*. New Haven, Yale University Press.

embedded in the stories which were actually recounted in the original language, especially in Ireland and the Scottish Highlands. As the culture of oral story-telling fragmented in parallel with the language, the stories were collected, translated where necessary, and published.[114] They were of course edited to meet the needs of a different audience and this change in targeted audience from a rural Cornish listener to an urban English reader changed the stories themselves.[115] The Cornish audience sought entertainment but also an affirmation of identity and community; the English audience diversion and relief from the alienation within their own society, produced by industrialization, social change and religious uncertainty. This mood generated a new wave of literary fantasy, by writers such as Lewis Carroll and George MacDonald, going on to William Morris and into the early twentieth century, and arguably into our own time. Much of this material draws on the folklore of the Victorian collectors, but it is accompanied by a sceptical attitude towards the folklore itself, hence the playful, ironic tone of many literary fantasies of the time. Nonetheless they helped to meet emotional and psychological needs which grew stronger as the century wore in. In a final act of appropriation, the cultures of defeated peoples were made to serve the purposes of the colonial power, to express the repressed impulses of the divided Victorian psyche, and conceal its own self-alienation.[116]

We should of course be grateful that the stories were collected and published, since they would otherwise have been irrecoverably lost, or buried in the bound transactions of obscure learned societies. We should not however ignore the significance of this shift from the spoken to the written word, which also mirrors the wider social shift in emphasis from the communal to the individual. In this process the stories were commodified, and we begin to move into the world of plaster leprechauns, Cornish pixies that bring good luck, and

114 See for instance Campbell, J. F. 1940 (1994). *More West Highland Tales*. Vols. 1 and 2. Edinburgh, Birlinn.
115 See David Blamires' paper "A Workshop of Editorial Practice". In Davidson, H. E. and Chaudhri, A. (eds) (2003). *A Companion to the Fairy Tale*. Woodbridge, D. S. Brewer, pp. 71-84.
116 See Miyoshi, M. (1909). *The Divided Self: A Perspective on the Literature of the Victorians*. London, University of London Press.

Arthurian lager adverts on television: as symbols become divorced from a living culture, so they are degraded.

Symbols in History

It may be that the principal function of symbolic thinking is to connect the individual's inner world with the outside world of cultural, social and historical experience: the Cornish stories were "popular tales told by the hearthside". This process is mediated through myth, folklore, social ritual and the sacramental aspects of religion, and perhaps also through the boundless creativity of language itself. These rituals of memory enact identity, and are perhaps the strongest safeguards against madness, assuming madness to be a lack of correspondence between the inner and outer worlds, when the symbol is split off from the object and the individual becomes alienated from reality and the capacity to symbolize is lost.

Ironically, as it destroyed Cornish culture, England appropriated the symbols and used its giants, kings and legends to enrich her own art and literature, and this involved some curious transitions. Tennyson's *Idylls of the King* embodied a pessimism which permeated the great achievements of Victorian England, and in the process Arthur was transformed from a Cornish resistance leader to a medieval English king.[117] Cornwall on the other hand was given a new identity as a tourist destination, different enough to be charming but not different enough to be threatening;[118] and folklore and legend had an important part to play in this. Similar developments occurred in all the Celtic countries: whole communities lost a living connection with their past, symbols lost their complexity and depth, ancient stories were mocked and denigrated, associated with poverty and failure. The process continues as living communities fragment into individuals on Facebook, desperately trying to connect. The creative power of symbols is lost, and the transition from oral folktale to book is the first step along this road.

117 Barszewski, S. L. (2000). *Myth and National Identity in Nineteenth Century Britain: The Legends of King Arthur and Robin Hood.* Oxford, Oxford University Press.

118 Westland, E. (ed) (1997). *Cornwall: The Cultural Construction of Place.* Penzance, Patten Press.

For Jung the wider significance of symbols was of the utmost importance.[119] He hypothesized layers of unconsciousness, the personal, relatively superficial stratum which contains material from individual experience, and a deeper, shared level, the "collective unconscious", a reservoir of "archetypal symbols", which are the language of folklore and myth. In the Cornish stories, Cherry's ointment and the giants' clubs can be seen as examples of this kind of symbol. This process of disintegration, already far advanced in the Celtic lands where it always met with resistance, has now spread widely in Anglo-American culture itself as family and cultural life fragment and the written and spoken word retreats in the face of media owned and manipulated by vested interests.

Instead of symbols rooted in historical experience we are presented with a banal kaleidoscope of shimmering images. In myth and legend though, we can still catch a glimpse of ourselves as we really are, as the western Celts saw their true reflection in their beautiful bronze mirrors upon which perched the owls of wisdom. Like mirrors books are tricky things which often say more and not infrequently less than their authors intend: a collection of stories which to one generation may be a quaint and amusing testimony to a picturesque, vanishing people may be to another a source of wisdom, hope and resistance. We have much to learn from the cruel punishment of Tregeagle, the gentle wisdom of Jowan Chy An Hor, the themes of loss and defiance which resonate through these stories which Hunt and Bottrell gathered so long ago. These are universal themes because they were originally shaped by a people which, while strongly Cornish in language and culture was also part of a wider Celtic and European tradition. They also present us with an opportunity to see how Cornish men and women, over countless generations, made sense of themselves and their world.

Late Cornish Literature

The story of the translation of Celtic language narratives into English rivals any of the stories themselves in its complexity and ambivalence, shaped as it was by a strange and shifting confluence

119 Jung, C. G. (1952). *Symbols of Transformation.* Collected Works, Vol. 5. London, Routledge and Kegan Paul.

of social, cultural and psychological forces. Early antiquarians such as William Stukeley in his work on stone and bronze age monuments provided an initial impetus towards a rediscovery of the "Celtic" past, and it is largely due to Stukeley that most people still associate Stonehenge, quite erroneously, with the Druids: the need to remember can sometimes lead us astray, and much of the work carried out at this time romanticized the past in order to meet the needs of the present.

In the late seventeenth and early eighteenth centuries a small group of Cornish gentlemen led by Nicholas and John Boson recorded fragments of the Cornish language, which was then in terminal decline, and even produced some original texts of their own, for didactic rather than literary purposes.[120] Nicholas, John and Thomas Boson wrote between 1660 and 1780, though their dates and precise relationships are unclear. They lived in and around Newlyn and belonged to a type of "gentleman-scholar" which was common in Britain at that time. Their scholarly interests, including the Cornish language, were the subject of correspondence with other learned men, such as William Gwavas. The Bosons themselves were not native speakers of Cornish, though they did learn it: they and their friends were essentially antiquarians, not revivalists, with a scholarly interest in preserving the scraps of Cornish which survived:

> In the Boson family we see a kind of last-ditch attempt to write a modern Cornish acquired only in the face of clear opposition.[121]

Their literary productions are clearly written for other scholars, and their "modernization" is designed to do that, not an attempt to enact communal memory. They are, in Brian Murdoch's phrase, "as much about the language as in it". Their most substantial work (it is not quite clear which of them wrote what) is the folktale "John of Chyanhor", which was probably written by John Boson. It is an international folktale about a St Levan man who seeks work in the

---

120 Padel, O. (1973). *The Cornish Writings of the Boson Family*. Redruth, Institute of Cornish Studies.
121 Murdoch, *op. cit.*, p. 132.

east and agrees to take three words of advice in lieu of wages: these words are i) never leave an old road for a new (*"komeer weeth na rea gara an voss goeth rag an vorr noueth"*), ii) never stay in a house where there is an old man with a young wife, and iii) not to act when angry.[122] By following this advice Jowan travels safely back to Lands End, acquiring wealth along the way

The story has much charm, and is still used as a teaching tool for learners. But a sadly typical theme of this literature is the death of the language itself, as in the graveyard elegy:

> Dadn an Mean, ma deskes brose dean
> En tavaz Kernooak Gelles.
> Termen vedn toaz, Rag an Corf the thoras
> Boz Tavaz Coth Kernow [eu] kelles.

> Under this stone a mighty learned one
> Is, in our Cornish language gone
> At the Great Assize his body will rise.
> Cornwall forgets her native tongue.[123]

This example shows that Cornish no longer has its own distinctive style, and is confined to weak imitations of English models; and as Nicholas Boson writes in "Nebbaz Gerriau dro tho Cornoack" ("A Few Words about Cornish"):

> Our Cornish tongue is so far weakened that we cannot hardly expect to see it grow again, for as did the English send it to this narrow land at first, thus it is still bearing upon it without leaving to it any place but about the cliff and the sea.[124]

For some, the work of the Bosons has formed the basis of a modern reconstructed Cornish language, though most revivalists have preferred to base their work on medieval "Middle Cornish" in which

---

122 Padel, *op. cit.*, pp. 14-24.
123 *Ibid.*, p. 48
124 *Ibid.*, p. 35.

most of the surviving literature is written.[125] The history of the language revival is itself a prodigious act of memory, the reconstruction of a broken mirror.

The Cornish Revival

The Cornish language revival began towards the end of the nineteenth century and was part of a wider re-invention which Philip Payton described as:

> a conscious project on the part of a small fraction of the Cornish middle class to solve the problems caused by the collapse of industrial Cornwall. Instead of focusing on the lost glories of steam engine technology this group began to look to a past when Cornwall was unashamedly "different" and more "Celtic".[126]

The revival was a romantic construction. The Cowethas Kelto-Kernuak (Cornish Celtic Society) was set up in 1901 in order to promote Cornwall's "Celtic Catholic heritage".[127] A founder member of the "Cowethas", Henry Jenner, published his *Handbook of the Cornish Language* in 1904 to provide not only a history and guide to the language but also a means of learning it, though he himself seems to have considered language revival impracticable,[128] and it may be doubted if anyone has ever learned to speak Cornish successfully from Jenner's *Handbook*. For him learning the language was an affirmation of identity, an affirmation to be achieved by a conscious act of remembrance:

---

125 See Payton, P. (1996). "Which Cornish? Ideology and Language Revival in Post-War Cornwall." In Nicgraith, M. (1996). *Watching One's Tongue: Aspects of Romance and Celtic Languages*. Liverpool, Liverpool University Press.
126 Deacon, B. and Payton, P. (1993). "Re-inventing Cornwall: Cultural Change on the European Periphery." In Payton, P (1993). *Cornish Studies 1*.
127 Payton, P. (2004). *Cornwall: A History*. Fowey, Cornwall Editions, p. 261.
128 See Jenner, H. (1904). *A Handbook of the Cornish Language*. David Nutt, London. (New edition Evertype, Cathair na Mart, 2010.) See also Williams, D. R. (ed) (2004) *Henry and Katherine Jenner. A Celebration of Cornwall's Culture, Language and Identity*. London, Francis Routle.

GATHERING THE FRAGMENTS

Most Cornishmen habitually speak English and few, very few, could hold five minutes conversation in the old Celtic speech. Yet the memory of it lingers on, and no-one can talk about the county itself, and mention the places in it without using a wealth of true Cornish words.[129]

Language evokes memory, and memory identity. This perspective looked beyond the Methodism and industrialism of the recent past to a "Celtic" pre-Reformation Cornwall, so linking up with the agenda of an emerging tourist industry.[130] Jenner was followed by Robert Morton Nance who devised a system called "Unified Cornish" based on the medieval texts. Since these texts are somewhat scanty he was obliged to supplement them with vocabulary borrowed from other Celtic languages, and a speculative phonology.[131] But unlike Jenner, Nance did envisage a revived language which might be "for all".

That Unified Cornish was a great achievement cannot be doubted though Nance's methods have always been subject to criticism, and in 1984 Glanville Price dismissed it as "pseudo-Cornish, Cornic" declaring that:

the old Celtic speech of Cornwall died out two centuries ago. It is still dead, and will evermore remain so.[132]

In the 1980s Ken George developed a criticism of Nance's "unified" language, concentrating on the phonological problem, that is, the inconsistency between Middle Cornish spelling and Late Cornish pronunciation.[133] He concluded that revived Cornish should be based on the surviving texts and an estimation of how the

129 Jenner, *op cit.*, p. 3.
130 Payton, P. (1992). *The Making of Modern Cornwall: Historical Experience and the Persistence of "Difference"*. Redruth, Dyllanson Truran, pp. 125-6.
131 Nance, R. M. (1929). *Cornish for All.* St Ives Federation of Old Cornwall Societies. See also Thomas, P. W. and Williams, D. R. (2007). *Setting Cornwall on its Feet: Robert Morton Nance.* London, Francis Boutle.
132 Price, G. (1984). *The Languages of Britain.* London, Edward Arnold.
133 George, K. (1986). *The Spelling and Pronunciation of Revived Cornish.* Torpoint, Cornish Language Board. See also Nicgraith, *op. cit.*, pp. 111-136.

46

language might have been pronounced around the year 1500, which is of course problematic. Nonetheless, in 1987 the Cornish Language Board accepted George's proposals and the new language was called *Kernewek Kemmyn* 'Common Cornish' which was for a time the most widely taught form of the language.

Out of this uncertainty arose *Kernuak*, or "Modern Cornish", a standardized version of Late Cornish, based on the latest known forms of Cornish from the 17th and 18th centuries from writers such as Nicholas Boson, John Boson, William Rowe, Thomas Tonkin, and others.[134] Richard Gendall, who pioneered Kernuak, felt that the pronunciation of the older generation of traditional (English) speakers in west Penwith was a reliable guide to the sounds of Late Cornish, though it is hard to see how this could be so since the Cornish language has not been spoken there for eight generations, and the sounds of southwestern English dialect have themselves changed over that time. Nonetheless as Philip Payton persuasively argued, Kernuak was an attempt to free the Cornish language from Nance's romantic ideology and to bridge the gap between modern speakers and the last generation to speak vernacular Cornish in the far west:

> There was emotional strength in this argument, providing a sense of historical closeness and continuity for contemporary learners, reassuring them that it was indeed "their" language, and a legitimate part of their personal inheritance.[135]

Payton argued that these different forms of the language, Unified, Kemmyn, and Kernuak expressed "deep-seated ideological contests" and this is doubtless true. The ideological contests though arise from the profound dislocations in historical continuity caused by the loss of the language itself and the traumas of industrialization and de-industrialization on top of the colonial experience itself. The

---

134 Gendall, R. (1991). *A Students' Grammar of Modern Cornish.* Cussel an Tavas Kernuack, Mahunyes, 1991.

135 Payton, P. (1992). *The Making of Modern Cornwall.* Redruth, Dyllanson Truran, p. 128.

language revival in its different forms is an attempt to rediscover identity through memory. According to Walter Benjamin:

> memory creates the chain of tradition which passes a happening on from generation to generation[136]

and this of course is mediated through language. The attempt to "remember" or reconstruct the language was an attempt to rediscover a lost identity, and the conflict over which form of the language to adapt is essentially a conflict over identity and it is probable that, given time and goodwill on all sides, the different forms of Cornish would eventually merge.

There have been signs of this rapprochement already. In a series of books Nicholas Williams criticized evident inaccuracies in George's reconstruction, both in terms of its phonology and its approach to English borrowings into traditional Cornish. (See Williams 1995, 2006a, 2006b, and Everson *et al.* 2007). This, combined with pressure from the Unified and Kernuak elements of the revival, gave rise to a consultation process out of which was devised a "compromise" orthography known as the Standard Written Form, published in 2008. A public group known as *Spellyans* 'Spelling' examined the SWF, and implemented a set of changes to it to correct evident errors and inconsistencies, called *Kernowek Standard*, 'Standard Cornish', in which a great many books have appeared since 2009.

The Uses of the Past

The age of the gentleman scholars was also the age of literary fraud, of Chatterton's spoof medieval verse and Ireland's "rediscovered" Shakespeare plays: it was a time when authors felt free to manipulate texts which were not established in the modern sense, and although we may be grateful for Purcell's lovely theatre music we may regret what Dryden did to *Anthony and Cleopatra* and *The Tempest*, not to mention his somewhat free treatment of Cornwall's own King Arthur.

136 Benjamin, W. (1973). *Illuminations*. London, Fontana.

These activities seem to be related to a sense of cultural superiority towards the past, which to the educated men of the Enlightenment (and they were, of course men), was associated with backwardness, irrationality and papist superstition (qualities which were also associated with women at the time). They had a very similar attitude towards the "Celtic" other, in Cornwall for instance, even as they appropriated its culture by publishing its texts.[137] On a deeper level this must surely indicate insecurity. The debt to the past is too substantial to be denied without threatening identity, but its acknowledgement is also risky, since it forces us to recognize that we are not self-created, which is an affront to our narcissism. We distort the past therefore to make it appear that it has always been ours: this is particularly true of American popular culture. In a recent film version of Dodie Smith's *A Hundred and One Dalmations* England is populated with racoons and beavers, in a recent example of cultural appropriation. So American filmgoers are protected from the nagging fear that the outside world may not in every respect resemble California. Similarly the eighteenth-century Englishmen knew that the outside world ought to resemble England, and when it failed to acquiesce it had to be recreated, or beaten into submission. On a literary level, later British scholars were to do the same thing to the Arthurian legend and the emancipatory working-class stories of Robin Hood.

James MacPherson, like Walt Disney, wanted to make money. In 1759 he circulated a number of texts which he claimed to have translated from old manuscripts in Scots Gaelic: this eventually led to the publication of "Fragments of Ancient Poetry", "Temora", and most famously "Fingal" in 1762. It would be difficult to overestimate the importance of these dreadful books, and any page turned at random will suffice to give their flavour:

---

137 These attitudes are still occasionally found though couched in somewhat different terms. It is interesting to note that in our own time too established classics are being rewritten or provided with sequels. See for example Kamel Daoud's sequel to Camus's *L'etranger*, *The Meursault Investigation* (One World Press).

O ruler of the flight of steel! My father
Hear thy son. Retire with Morven's mighty
Chief! Give me the fame of Ossian. If here
I fail, O chief of my love, the white-handed
Daughter of Toscar. For, with red cheek
From the rock, bending over the stream
Her soft hair flies about her bosom.[138]

and so on and so forth.

All these flowing bosoms and what-not exercised a decisive influence on the growing Romantic movement, and such important figures as Herder, Goethe and even Blake acknowledged a debt to *Ossian*.[139] It is said that Napoleon carried a copy of *Ossian* to his dying day.

MacPherson claimed that he based his works on ancient Gaelic manuscripts, but his claims are doubtful, to say the least of it. His genius however lay not in scholarship but in his ability to shape those elements of the Gaelic tradition with which he was familiar into narratives which, to an extraordinary extent, expressed the yearnings and fantasies of his own time and social class. But he has nothing to tell us about the real tradition, or about the people who created and sustained it.

And in this, though he could not have known it at the time, MacPherson began a tradition of his own. Many writers, including Rousseau in his myth of the "noble savage"(which may have influenced *Ossian*), going back to Caesar and Heradotus, have simplified and exploited cultures distant in space and time in order to promote their own agendas; but MacPherson was the first to use a Celtic culture for such purposes: he was not to be the last, and Queen Victoria and her followers later made astute use of such fragments of Gaeldom as survived down to their time to develop a nineteenth century myth of Scottishness in support of the British monarchy, which survives in an attenuated form into our own

138 MacPherson, J. (1876). *The Poems of Ossian*. Edinburgh, A and C Black.
139 See Black, G. F. (1926). "MacPheron's 'Ossian' and the Ossianic Controversy".
Bulletin of the New York Public Library 30. And Stafford, J (1988) *The Sublime Sauage: James MacPherson and the Poems of Ossian*. Edinburgh, Edinburgh University Press.

time.[140] MacPherson certainly made the wider European audience aware of "Celtic" literature but only by falsifying the tradition itself, as translation, not to mention deliberate falsification, must inevitably do. This could only happen because of the low status of the tradition itself in comparison with the imperial, English-speaking culture in which it was subsumed. Though no Cornish texts ever had the impact of *Ossian* or anything like it, they too had to be appropriated by the imperial project, and this process of course paralleled the expropriation of territory and markets which was proceeding rapidly. These developments affirmed Anglo-Saxon hegemony and allayed growing anxieties about imperial overstretch, miscegenation, economic competition and religious doubt, which accumulated as the century progressed. The Victorians read the past in terms of conquest and competition, since that was their own model.[141] It is therefore self-evident that the victory of English over Cornish and the other Celtic languages was a good thing.

Other cultures too were made to serve the imperial dream and the process of cultural appropriation at home corresponded with colonial expansion overseas, as British museums grew fat with imperial loot and British libraries with expropriated literature and legends. The most attractive examples aimed at a wider readership were published early in the twentieth century by George Harrap and the Gresham Publishing Company. These include T. W. Rolleston's *Myths and Legends of the Celtic Race* (Harrap, 1911) and Charles Squire's *Celtic Myth and Legend, Poetry and Romance* (Gresham, no date). These volumes were beautifully bound and illustrated in a romantic style by the likes of C. Wallcousins, H. R. Miller, G. F. Watts and Ford Madox Brown. Such books made a significant contribution to the literary and artistic culture of the time, feeding into the movement which became known as "The Celtic Twilight" from the title of Yeats' book, which was most strongly felt in Ireland where it produced a major literature, still associated with Lady Gregory,

---

140 Hobsbawn, E. and Ranger, T. (eds) (1983). *The Invention of Tradition.* Cambridge, Cambridge University Press, pp. 15-42.
141 See for instance Wawn, A. (2000). *The Vikings and the Victorians: Inventing the Old North in Nineteenth Century Britain.* Woodbridge, D. S. Brewer.

George Russell, and Yeats himself.[142] Much of this was inspired by folklore and translated texts.

Nothing like Yeats' Abbey Theatre emerged in Cornwall, though Robert Morton Nance in his Cornu-English Cledry Plays did attempt to put some of the folklore of west Cornwall into a popular dramatic format, and these plays did lead to the foundation of the first Old Cornwall Society.[143] The subtitle, "Drolls of Old Cornwall: for Village Acting and Home Reading", suggests a desire to bring the community together in a shared celebration of story and dialect.

Language Studies

With the nineteenth century came the rise of historical philology. Franz Bopp first proved that Celtic was a member of the Indo-European group of languages, and Kaspar Zeuss's *Grammatica Celtica*, published in 1851, represented the true beginning of Celtic Studies as a distinct discipline. The first scholarly journals were the French *Revue Celtique* in 1870 and the *Zeitschrift für Celtische Philologie* in Germany. At the same time scholarly interest in folklore and mythology was growing rapidly, leading to the famous debate between Max Müller and Andrew Lang which was to enliven the pages of the learned reviews. But as early as 1835 the Scot Hugh Miller expressed the fear that:

> the stream of tradition was rapidly lessening, and that oral knowledge of the past would soon be lost.[144]

142 Yeats, W. B. (1895, reprinted 1987). *The Celtic Twilight.* Gerrards Cross, Colin Smythe.
143 Kent, T. A., *op. cit.*, p. 158. Nance, R. M. (1956). *The Cledry Plays: Drolls of Old Cornwall for Village Acting and Home Reading.* Federation of Old Cornwall Societies.
144 Miller, H. (1935). *Scenes and Legends of the North of Scotland.* Edinburgh, A. and C. Black.

Chapter 4

The Uses of the Past

Texts and Stories

In the *Atheneum* the Englishman W. J. Thoms, now considered the founder of modern folkloristics, appealed for help:

> I am not without hopes of enlisting your aid in garnering the few ears which are remaining, scattered over that field from which our forefathers might have gathered a goodly crop. No-one who has made the manners, customs, observances, superstitions, ballads, proverbs and etc of the olden times his study, but must have arrived at two conclusions: the first, how much that is curious and interesting in these matters is now entirely lost; the second, how much may yet be rescued by timely exertion.[145]

This elegiac tone is to be found throughout the nineteenth century with regard to folklore, not least in Cornwall, where Robert Hunt described it as "a wreck upon the ocean". It resembles in some respects the attitude taken by editors towards the early Cornish texts and the Celtic languages generally, though they tend to be even more dismissive. Even Mathew Arnold, in a caricature of "the poor Welshman" says:

> his land is a province, and his history petty, and his Saxon subduers scout his speech as an obstacle to civilisation, and the echo of all its kindred in other lands is growing every day fainter and more feeble, gone in Cornwall, going in Brittany and the Scottish Highlands, going too in Ireland, and there

---

145 Dorson, R. M. (1973). *America in Legend: Folklore from the Colonial Period to the Present.* New York, Pantheon.

above all, the badge of the beaten race, the property of the vanquished.[146]

Arnold often explored loss through his poetry, the death of the Norse gods in *Balder Dead*, and "the melancholy, long, withdrawing roar" of the Sea of Faith in the superb *Dover Beach*.[147] The so-called "death of God" was a key theme in later Victorian poetry, and in the mind-set of the time. This curious idea had taken root long before Darwin and was probably related to the Industrial Revolution and the social changes which accompanied it, creating the delusion that man had finally mastered the natural world. Not least in Cornwall, as the old language faded away it became harder to believe in the Tory, Anglican God, and the impression that this God was on the side of a reactionary aristocracy did not make him popular. This led many to search for new forms of belief, or to revive older ones, most notably the famous *Tracts for the Times* in 1833 which led to the Oxford Movement and the conversion of Newman to the Catholic church.[148] The Oxford Movement revived interest in the medieval world and influenced both literature (through Tennyson and Morris) and art, particularly the pre-Raphaelites. It also reinforced the Gothic tendencies of A. W. Pugin and other architects.[149]

The Cornish revival therefore took place against a background in which England's own relationship with the past had been seriously disrupted, and this produced a widespread malaise, leading sometimes to despair. A character in *Robert Elsmere*, a novel of "faith and doubt", by Mathew Arnold's niece Mrs Humphrey Ward, recalls that he first became aware when at university:

> Of something cold, impotent and baffling in himself, which was to stand forever between him and action, between him

146 Arnold, M. (1867), reprinted 1919. *On the Study of Celtic Literature and Other Essays*. London, J. M. Dent, pp. 15-16.
147 See Macbeth (ed) (1969). *Victorian Verse*. London, Penguin.
148 See Faber, G. (1933). *Oxford Apostles: A Character Study of the Oxford Movement*. Harmondsworth, Penguin.
149 See Hill, R. (2007). *God's Architect: Pugin and the Building of Romantic Britain*. London, Allen Lane.

and human affection, the growth of the critical pessimist sense which laid the axe to the root of enthusiasm, friendship after friendship—which make other men feel him inhuman, intangible, a skeleton at the feast; and the persistence through it all of a kind of hunger for life and its satisfactions which the will was more and more powerless to satisfy.

And similar feelings were expressed by Pater, Kingsley, Carlyle and countless others.[150]

Cornwall and Britain

The contribution of Cornish culture to the Victorian project became clearer as the century wore on, though it was never crucial. The cult of King Arthur and the Knights of the Round Table served to legitimize monarchical rule and the public school ethos which bound the ruling class together. It also allowed access to an idealized Middle Ages and helped to bridge the huge cultural divide which the Industrial Revolution had opened up, if only in fantasy. It also buttressed the cult of hero worship which grew to astounding proportions in the course of the nineteenth century and helped to compensate for a growing sense of powerlessness and for a certain flattening of individuality which a mercantile democracy inevitably produced. The stories of Arthur and Tristan fed into a medieval fantasy England and the publication of Cornish literary texts provided support for British academics against their French and German competitors. Mathew Arnold's comparative study of Celtic literature led to a Celtic Studies Chair at Oxford. His *Tristram and Iseult* was the first poetic reworking of the story in English.

Translation is itself a form of appropriation and in Cornwall's case it is paralleled by the economic exploitation which went on at an astounding rate throughout the century. The looting of Cornwall's natural resources was a pilot project for imperial exploitation across the globe, a Promethean vision of unbridled capitalism. At the same time improved transport and economic integration strengthened the illusion that Cornwall was a part of England, albeit with an

---

150 Houghton, W. E. (1957). *The Victorian Frame of Mind 1830-1870*. New Haven, Yale University Press.

innocuous sense of difference, enough to make it a suitable holiday destination.[151] Even Hunt's great collection of stories was called *Popular Romances of the West of England.*

From the safety of his study Sir James Frazer produced: *The Golden Bough*, a vast attempt to codify and explain away the "observances and superstitions" of the simple-minded people who believed or had once believed them. That their understanding of such observances might have been deeper or more complex than his own did not of course occur to him. For Frazer, as for most contemporary scholars, folk beliefs and narratives were simply the result of ignorance. Some of them scarcely bothered to conceal their contempt. From our point of view this Comtean positivism seems simpleminded in itself, though it was a basic assumption at the time.

The Advance of Celtic Studies

The study and translation of surviving Celtic texts was paralleled by the study and publication of Celtic folklore, and stemmed from the same psychological roots, though in both cases what survived can only have been a tattered remnant of what once had been, and as in the case of Thoms above workers in the field often spoke in language which was tinged with irreparable loss. Following the work of Zeuss, a first Chair of Celtic Studies was created at Oxford in 1877, and was filled by the great John Rhys.[152] A steady stream of translations from Irish and Welsh literature (which have always been the main focus of Celtic Studies) was produced by a line of the scholars, especially Kuno Meyer and the Irishmen Whitley Stokes and J. G. O'Keefe, translator of *Buile Suibhne.* Whitley Stokes also translated the Cornish *Poem of the Passion* in 1860, following an earlier translation by Davies Gilbert in 1826, and the *Creation of the World* in 1864.[153] The *Ordinalia* was translated and edited by Edwin Norris in 1859.

151 See Deacon, B. "The Hollow arring of the Distant Steam Engines: Images of Cornwall between West Barbary and Delectable Duchy." In Western, E. (1997). *Cornwall: The Cultural Construction of Place.* Penzance, Patten Press.

152 Parry Williams, J. (1954). *John Dreys 1840-1915.* Cardiff, University of Wales Press. Sir John's old study now houses the magnificent Celtic Library in Jesus College.

153 See Royle, E. and Russell, P. (eds) (2010). *The Tripartite Life of Whitley Stokes.* Dublin, Four Courts Press.

Some popular tales have escaped from their academic confines. W. B. Yates for instance was especially influenced by the tales of Cú Chulain, which he turned into such plays as *On Baile's Strand* and *The Green Helmet* which were produced at the Abbey Theatre in the first decade of the twentieth century.[154] Ancient story was transformed into a new art form for a new state, and indeed helped to created the new state, and Yeats agonized in verse about whether his "Countess Cathleen" had driven the rebels to their death in 1916. To this day a statue of the Hound of Ulster stands in the Dublin GPO to celebrate the Easter Rising, such is the power of memory and narrative. Stories can be used for either reactionary or emancipatory purposes, as the history of the biblical narrative demonstrates.

The development of Celtic Studies was part of a wider revolution in higher education which was made possible by economic growth and which had the universities to introduce courses in modern history, natural and social sciences, art (thanks to Ruskin) and modern literatures from the 1860s onwards.[155] Folklore itself was beginning to turn into a science and Hunt's *Popular Romances* was the first large scale survey of the kind which has since become standard. The most influential early collection was the *Kinder und Hausmärchen* ('Children's and Household Tales') by the Grimm brothers, an anthology of traditional stories published in two volumes between 1812 and 1815.[156] In an increasingly nationalistic Europe folklore was thought to embody the distinctive ethos of the people and to provide evidence for its historic continuity, though it also revealed the similarities between different cultures. In its extreme nationalist form it became a significant factor in Heinrich Himmler's racist ideology, but this was in the distant future. For now the folktales of dispossessed peoples were being translated into the dominant language and published to strengthen the unity of the national state, a paradoxical strengthening of solidarity in an increasingly competitive and insurrectionary Europe.

154 Fitz-Simon, C. (2003). *The Abbey Theatre: Ireland's National Theatre. The First Hundred Years.* New York, Thames and Hudson.
155 Houghton, W. E., *op. cit.*, p. 142.
156 See Georges, R. A. and Jones, M. O. (eds) (1995). *Folkloristics: An Introduction.* Bloomington, Indiana University Press, pp. 31-57.

Expansion was seen in all the physical and social sciences, and the rise of materialism and positivism led to reductionist integrations in many fields: folklorists often felt obliged to apologize for their work. The question of literal truth had begun to arise, and had been turned into a moral judgement which undermined the self-belief of the storyteller and his or her audience. As the "guidwife" says at the beginning of Hunt's Cornish collection:

> "There were plenty of people that could tell these stories once. I used to hear them telling them over the fire at night: but people is so changed with pride now that they care for nothing."[157]

This speech signals the decline of oral tradition. Almost exactly a hundred years later, and in a different context David Thomson captures the precise moment of the death.[158] Thomson is on Uist and has been listening to the old people tell of the seals who are able to weep and speak like human beings, when a young woman takes him aside:

> "It is all lies," she said, "you know well it is lies."
> "What do you mean, Mairi?"
> "It is well for you to come and ask about the seals, and away home with you then to the mainland."
> "But I don't think of the stories that way—as lies or truth. I like to hear them, that's all."
> She stared.
> "Like reading a western?"
> "Perhaps."
> "The old people believe them."
> "Well, I don't see any harm in that, do you?"
> "On the mainland they wouldn't believe them."
> "No."
> "Not even the old people?"

157 Hunt, *op. cit.*
158 Thomson, D. (1954). *The People of the Sea*. Edinburgh, Canongate, p. 161.

"Very few of them would. But they believe lots of other things just as strange."

"They are not backward in the mainland. O, I wish I could go there to work!"

This notion of backwardness versus progress, rationalistic and value laden as it is, is the legacy of the Victorian era, and it is not dead yet. The belief in irreversible progress, though it would be falsified at Auschwitz, was only partly to do with scientific advance. In large part:

> It was a metaphysical conception of the universe erected on the narrow foundation of natural evolution. By 1850 the evidence of palaeontology made it possible to read the history of animal life as a great progressive development from the amoeba up through fishes to reptiles, to birds, to mammals, culminating—so far—in man. But need it stop there?[159]

And "man" himself of course was arranged in a hierarchy of value, with Anglo-Saxon men at the top, and inferior breeds lower down (women of course are nowhere to be seen, save as the domestic "Angel in the House". Celtic peoples, for instance, were regarded as sharing certain characteristics with women and children (irrationality, labile emotions, inconsistency and unreliability) and these perceptions filtered down to the Celtic communities themselves, as in the example above, producing a cultural fracture which divided the generations, and separated young people from their past. The mirror of tradition cracked, and people could no longer recognize their own image in the glass: when a rich and powerful culture encounters a small and powerless one, such negative judgements become internalized and create a sense of inferiority. Mairi, in the story above does not perhaps like "the old people" much, but she doesn't like herself much either, stranded as she is between two cultures; and this situation must have been enacted countless times

159 Houghton, *op. cit.*, p. 36.

in the Celtic countries, not least in Cornwall, in the unequal clash
between modernity and tradition.

Emigration

Stories told in the Gaelic language were of course even more at risk
than tales told in English in Cornwall, since their communities were
decimated by the potato famines which had swept through both
Scotland and Ireland, and by the Highland clearances: one can only
speculate as to how much traditional narrative had already been
lost.[160] The uncontrolled expansion of manufacturing in Britain and
North America and the global development of mining also sucked
the people out of their heartlands, simultaneously weakening and
devaluing the inherited way of life of those who remained. But also
systematic attempts were made to liquidate or appropriate the most
conspicuous signs of difference, particularly language in the interests
of homogeneity. The "nation states" which emerged at the
Renaissance were in effect pilot projects for the great global empires
of the nineteenth century. Mathew Arnold was not the only one to
rejoice at the passing of Cornish.

Though some of these distinctive features lingered on in the
transported communities which settled in the new urban centres, it
became increasingly clear that the only future for the Celt was as
part of the English-speaking imperium. A few charming idio-
syncrasies. piskies, kilts. leprechauns and the like were allowed to
persist, but authentic tradition must be confined to the past, in part
by the collection of folktales and the publication of old texts. The
wild forces of Celtic identity had to be corralled in the pages of *Revue
Celtique* or children's stories—the association between women,
children and uneducated or "primitive" people in Victorian culture
deserves a study in itself. Arnold genuinely loved Celtic storytelling
so long as it stayed in the study where it belonged. That the death of
Welsh might be "a practical inconvenience" to those who spoke it,
or that the death of "the last Cornish peasant who spoke the old
tongue" might cause more than "a moment's distress" in Cornwall

160 Though Cornwall itself suffered from the potato blight in the 1840s, and there
were fifteen occasions of widespread food rioting between 1729 and 1847.
Deacon, *op. cit.*, p. 125.

THE USES OF THE PAST

itself did not occur to him.[161] Though the "scholar gypsy" himself might experience a romantic frisson of regret all that really mattered was "to become more thoroughly one with the rest of the country". This of course begs a question: if Cornwall was "one with the rest of the country", why did it have a different language in the first place? Because the languages did not fit the new imperial paradigm they had to be wiped out. And this was no mere academic exercise as generations of beaten and humiliated Welsh- and Gaelic-speaking children could testify. This must have generated thousands of intergenerational conflicts even more painful than Mairi's in Thomson's story—as whole peoples were defrauded of their memories.

This was deliberate policy designed to produce a single market and a single state, with a single language and religion. It was not entirely successful in destroying national distinctiveness, as the recent successes of Scottish nationalism show.

The Empire of Knowledge

Despite the recognition of Cornish as a minority language by the European Union and the interest generated by the language controversy, not to mention the brave efforts of language activists, there are probably no more than a few hundred Cornish speakers at present. Nonetheless, there has been much progress in education and public awareness, and Cornish words are widely used. There is a growing belief that the different forms of the language and mutually reconcilable.

> The language movement increasingly sees these forms as skin to dialects, as indeed modern English has both regional dialects and different official forms, which pose few problems today. The language institutions are developing mutual recognition and ways of working together. Kemmyn and Unified users frequently testified that only spelling really distinguishes them. Users of Unified and modern/late

161 Arnold, M. (1967) (1910) *On the Study of Celtic Literature.* London, J. M. Dent.

Cornishes speak of the ways in which their speech varieties are becoming closer together.[162]

It seems likely that, given adequate resources and support, the different forms of Cornish would eventually become one (the language seems originally to have had northern and southern dialects) and the ideological rifts underlying them would heal. This would create a language that could truly mirror the Cornish experience, now and in the future.[163] This would be a constructive act of remembering.

The explosion of textual translation and folklore collection arose from the Victorian desire to map and therefore master the world, in psychological terms an infantile desire for omnipotence, an attempt to deny the fear of what is outside, different, other. But on the other hand, many individual scholars wanted to preserve at least the memory of traditions which they themselves loved. In a similar spirit museums and display cabinets in country rectories were stuffed with examples of flora and fauna which were becoming extinct in the wild. Plants and seeds flooded into Kew and Charles Darwin's house at Down, where they were classified and labelled to become part of Britain's global intellectual empire. Even extinct species were not immune as competition grew to identify and classify prehistoric animals. The self-confidence of Victorian science was staggering though often misconceived as in Richard Owen's reconstruction of dinosaurs for the permanent exhibition at the Crystal Palace at Sydenham.[164]

In this field as in others there was a fundamental ambivalence in Victorian thought. The more Victorians appropriated the world economically and intellectually, the more insecure they seemed to feel. Though the fossil discoveries at Lyme Regis affirmed their science they undermined their faith, since they appeared to contradict the account of creation in the Book of Genesis. The

162 MacKinnon, K. (2005). "Development of Cornish Language and Literature." In O'Neill (ed) (2005). *Rebuilding the Celtic Languages: Reversing Language Shift in the Celtic Countries.* Talybont, Y Lolfa.

163 See Lobb, J. and Ansell, G. (2004). *Strateji rag an Tavas Kernewek.* Truro, Cornwall County Council.

164 Cadbury, D. (2001). *The Dinosaur Hunters.* London, Fourth Estate.

intense academic rivalries evoked by "dinomania" seemed to mirror the rivalries between species in the natural world, past and present (Tennyson wrote of "nature red in tooth and claw") which were increasingly revealed by science, and faith began to seem a less reliable defence against despair. Victorian England became a zoo where the living and the dead mingled, as on the façade of Alfred Waterhouse's wonderful Natural History Museum; and though attempts were made to psychologically accommodate the new discoveries,[165] more sensitive people explored their disturbing implications, as John Martin did in his depiction of "The Country of the Iguanodon" in 1838.

The showpiece of the need to acquire and classify was of course the Great Exhibition of 1851 in Joseph Paxton's magnificent Crystal Palace, and widely seen as a celebration of British supremacy in the arts and sciences. Apart from the sheer number and variety of the manufactures on display, visitors were impressed by the huge effort which had gone into classifying them:

> An attempt was made also to impose internal order on the multitude of exhibits on display, objects which were classified, catalogued, illustrated, commented upon (even by people who had not seen them), often controversially, sometimes satirically. Classifying, itself controversial, was a favourite as well as a necessary Victorian preoccupation, like naming and listing.[166]

This large scale public collection and categorization was balanced on the domestic level. As the century wore on middle class houses filled with clutter, clumsy furniture and silverware, ornaments and nicknacks, including the first souvenirs from Cornwall and tours of the continent, signs of social status and conspicuous consumption. In an increasingly materialist culture possessions came to signify a person's wealth and standing, and after Ruskin, the kind of person one actually was. This was often reflected in the art of the time. In

165 By holding a dinner party inside the Iguanodon at Crystal Palace for instance. (*Illustrated London News*, 1854.)
166 Briggs, A. (2003). *Victorian Things*. Stroud Sutton Publishing, p. 37.

Holman Hunt's *The Awakening Conscience* for instance, the sensuous fabrics and ornamentation convey a powerful sense of wealth and sophistication as well as corruption.[167]

Of course this kind of obsessional behaviour (the need to possess and classify) is often an asset, in scientific research for instance, or any occupation requiring self-discipline and routine, and there is little doubt that Victorian society put a premium on the obsessional personality—one need only look at Darwin. But obsessionality also wastes a lot of energy and can cause serious mental disorder, and this type of neurosis was identified by Freud as one of the major frames of reference in psycho-analytic practice:

> In the most typical form of obsessional neurosis, the psychical conflict is expressed through symptoms which are described as compulsive obsessive ideas, compulsions towards undesirable acts, struggles against these thoughts and tendencies, exorcistic rituals etc and through a mode of thinking which is characterised in particular by rumination, doubt and scruples, and which leads t inhibitions of thought and action.[168]

That is to say, obsessional behaviour is a defence against unacceptable impulses and anxieties. Much has been made of sexual repression in Victorian England, and many would agree with Ronald Pearsall's summary that

> The basic attitude towards sexual matters of the middle classes was compounded of fear and alarm and shame.[169]

On the other hand there is evidence that many men and women led rich and fulfilling sexual lives in Victorian England.[170] But the

167 Tate Gallery, London.
168 Laplanche, J. and Pontalis, J. B. (eds) (1988). *The Language of Psychoanalysis.* London, Hogarth Press and The Institute of Psychoanalysis, p. 201.
169 Pearsall, R. (1969). *The Worm in the Bud: The World of Victorian Sexuality.* London, Weidenfect and Nicholson, pp. 628-9.
170 See Gay, P. (1984). *The Bourgeois Experience: Victoria to Freud.* Oxford, Oxford University Press.

emphasis on purity, especially for woman, "the angel in the house", did permeate society, and ensure that much sexual activity and even desire did arouse guilt and anxiety. Other powerful anxieties arose from religious doubt, political unrest and alienation. Of course, the need to accumulate capital and acquire colonies and markets provoked resistance and competition overseas, which justified racism. The thief must despise his victim to justify his theft.

Language and Empire

During this period too the Celtic languages were being studied, codified and classified. Though the relationship between the continental and insular Celtic languages had been understood in the sixteenth century the rise of historical philology did not begin until the first half of the nineteenth when Bopp proved that "Celtic" belonged to the Indo-European group and was therefore related to the classical Germanic and Sanscrit languages.[171] Zeuss's *Grammatica Celtica* in 1853 was the first scholarly overview of the Celtic languages, and Cornish thus took its place as an Indo-European Celtic language, alongside Welsh and Breton. Though this work was of great scholarly importance it has a rather melancholy feel, like that of the folklorists, given the increasingly parlous state of the languages themselves, as if the bones were being gathered for the great museum of dead languages which the world was shortly to become. As if, in Robert Hunt's words:

> We gather a fragment here and a fragment there, and at length, it may be, we learn something of the name and character of the vessel when it was freighted with life, and obtain a shadowy image of the people who have perished.[172]

The Victorians tended to see early history in terms of invasion and the conquest of inferior races and languages by superior ones, because this model reflected their own imperial strategies in Africa and Asia. In this model Cornwall was the first colony now, it was

171 Maier, B. (1997). *Dictionary of Celtic Religion and Culture.* Woodbridge Boydell Press, p. 66.
172 Hunt, *op. cit.*, p. 82.

believed, successfully incorporated into the mother country. As the English overthrew the Celts so, it was thought, waves of tall, blond Celts had overthrown the short, dark aboriginal inhabitants of Britain. This dynamic model is well represented by John Rhys's Rhind lectures in archaeology, delivered in December 1889.[173] In recent decades a different model has emerged, with large scale invasions replaced by small groups of immigrants and artisans who caused scarcely a ripple in the genetic pool.[174] The Celtic identity itself is seen as a late nineteenth century construct: notions of language and ethnicity combined to blur the identity issue and serve the nationalistic, imperialistic agendas of the time, though this does not change the fact that the Cornish community for instance had a strong and historically rooted sense of identity. The romantic fiction of the Celts recently shown never to have existed in the nineteenth century sense was designed to meet English needs.

Appropriating the Unconscious

A short time later Freud both colonized and mapped the unconscious uncovering its desires and anxieties and forcing it to see itself in the mirror of psychoanalysis. At the same time he laid the foundations of an imperialistic science which claimed to interpret the world. Freud analysed people and symptoms but also texts. So far as folktales were concerned, his main interest was in using them to illustrate his psychological theories, and many critics have used his theories to illuminate the stories. He noted the dreamlike quality of some folktales, and just as he interpreted his clients' dreams to uncover their neurotic conflicts and effect a cure so he decoded folktales in order to uncover what he considered to be universal psychological phenomena.[175] His followers, both folklorists and psychoanalysts like Otto Rank developed his ideas and Jung changed the emphasis from psychopathology to archetypal symbolism, in ways that have proved popular ever since.[176]

173 Rhys, J. (1990) reprint. *The Early Ethnology of the British Isles*. Felinfach, Llanerch.
174 See Chapman, M. (1992). *The Celts: The Construction of the Myth*. And James, S. (1999). *The Atlantic Celts: Ancient People or Modern Invention?* London, British Museum Press.
175 Freud, S. (1900) (reprinted 1954). *The Interpretation of Dreams*. Allen and Unwin.
176 See Zipes, J. (2000). *The Oxford Companion to Fairy Tales*. Oxford, Oxford

All this can throw much light on the folktale, and it is easy to interpret, say, "Cherry of Zennor" or the giant stories in terms of Oedipal theory. Indeed, the stories would presumably not have been told at all if they had not been consistent with the deeper truisms of human nature. This interpretive method is interesting enough, as far as it goes, if a little mechanical. It is though rather hard to see the point of demonstrating what is assumed to be a universal truth to begin with. There are problems with this: the first concerns the intellectual status of the theory itself.

Psychoanalysis is fundamentally based on the myth of Oedipus, though Freud developed the idea in his *Three Essays*. That is to say, the theory depends on the notion of the son's desire to supplant the father. On the 15th of October 1897 Freud wrote to his friend Fliess about his extraordinary discovery:

> If the (self) analysis fulfils what I expect of it, I shall work it out systematically and then put it before you. So far I have found nothing completely new, just all the complications to which I have become accustomed. It is by no means easy. Being totally honest with oneself is a good exercise. A single idea of general value dawned on me. I have found, in my own case too, the phenomenon of "being in love" with my mother and jealous of my father, and I now consider it a universal event in early childhood... If this is so, we can understand the gripping power of "Oedipus Rex" in spite of all the objections that reason raises against the presupposition of fate: and we can understand why the later "drama of fate" was bound to fail so miserably... the Greek legend seized upon a compulsion which everyone recognised because he senses its existence within himself. Everyone in the audience was once a budding Oedipus in fantasy and each recoils in horror from the dream fulfilment here translated into reality, with the full quantity of repression which separated his infantile state from his present one.[177]

University Press, pp. 404-8.

177 Masson, J. M. (1985). *The Complete Letters of Sigmund Freud to Wilhelm Eliott 1887-1904*. Cambridge Ma, Harvard University Press.

Oedipus therefore arose out of Freud's self-analysis. (Though all other analysts at the time and since were required to be analysed by another analyst Freud alone psychoanalysed himself.) It was "a single idea of general value" which dawned on him, though, as he implies he had encountered clinical material which led to the same conclusion. The leap from this essentially personal insight, however brilliant to "a universal event in early childhood", and from that to Sophocles, is less clear. When Freud claims that "everyone in the audience was once a budding Oedipus", we can only regard this as a poetic insight, though this is not to deny its validity as such. Since the audience does not presumably consist entirely of his own patients, he cannot know that they all have an Oedipus complex. Though brave attempts have been made by Freud's followers to demonstrate the universality of Oedipus, in cultures as remote from nineteenth century Vienna as the native peoples of central Australia, the results have been inconclusive and the proposition is probably untestable.[178]

Nor would anybody now be interested in testing it. Malinowski, the great pioneer of functionalism famously asserted the non-existence of the Oedipus complex among matrilineal peoples, such as those inhabiting the Trobriand Islands, but he was challenged by Freud's disciple Ernest Jones.[179] So the internal world was mapped and expropriated in parallel with the external one, and its language too was recorded, translated and preserved, just as Cornish was. Psychoanalysis itself might be described as an attempt to remember what has been deliberately forgotten, or repressed. It has helped many people to understand and resolve their neurotic difficulties, and has also contributed to our understanding of folklore, and helped us to take it more seriously instead of dismissing them as the childish productions of "primitive" people, as was once the case. It also provided insights which helped to undermine middle class culture, revealing its cynicism and hypocrisy, revealing new artistic possibilities.

178 Roheim, G. (1974). *Children of the Desert: The Western Tribes of Central Australia*. New York, Basic Books.
179 See Malinowski, B. (1926). "The Role of Myth in Life". In *London Psyche* 24. And Dunders, A. (1984). *Sacred Narrative: Readings in the Theory of Myth*. Berkeley, University of California Press.

But it also came to play an important part in upholding that culture, since to interpret is also to control and expropriate. The theoretical discourse is privileged at the expense of the patient or storyteller, who may have their own ways of understanding the world: though the purpose of psychoanalysis and the therapies which derive from it is to help the subject comprehend and take control of her own life. It also sets up a power relationship by demanding that the subject abandon his own narrative and accept that of the analyst. This process resembles translation, the change from an oral to a textual tradition: they are both changes in ownership.

Just as Freud appropriated the narratives of his patients to mine the unconscious and produce a theory which claimed to interpret the world, so vast tracts of land were being acquired overseas by Britain and the other western powers. And the Celtic regions were being opened up by the railways, their natural resources ripped from the earth. Both these processes began late in the eighteenth century, Freud's theory providing the capstone late in the nineteenth. Both developments stemmed from the same psychological/economic need to dominate. This development inevitably hastened the destruction of the indigenous languages, a crime of historic proportions.

The Golden Age

As Britain was transformed by the Industrial Revolution and its consequences the political and psychological need for homogeneity and control became acute. People experienced anxiety at the loss of familiar landscapes and ways of life, because such losses are a threat to memory and identity. As contemporary folk songs attest ("I can't find Brummagem") the world, in less than a lifetime, had become a strange and frightening place for millions.

This led to nostalgic "revivals" of folksong and dance in England as much as it fed a burgeoning "Celtic" romanticism: hence the invention of "Merrie England":

A cultural ideal which located the remedy for the evils of modern life in a golden age found sometime in the late medieval or Tudor era... People of many different ideological persuasions looked back lovingly to an agrarian past when institutions such as the manor or the village bound men together in relationships, strengthened by mutual interests and affections.[180]

The Robin Hood ballads were made to fit this idealized version of the past. William Morris championed a return to medieval aesthetics, prompted by what he saw as the shoddy ugliness of industrial production, and ended up a revolutionary socialist.[181] This sensibility affected late Victorian art and architecture, where it often carried a similar radical implication, with regard to the present.[182] In his celebrated "Contrasts" for instance, earlier in the century, Pugin had compared medieval architecture with contemporary style to the disadvantage of the latter, and in one of the plates he added to the second edition of 1841 he specifically contrasted the "Catholic town" of 1440 with the soulless industrial town of the 1840s.[183]

By mid-Victorian times, the past invoked by the demure revivals of Maypoles and rush bearing was too vague to be capable of any precise chronological location. But the attributes of Merry England were constant: a contented revelling peasantry, and a hierarchical order in which each one happily accepted his place and where the feast in the baronial hall symbolised the ideal social relationship.[184]

Such a perspective of course denies both class conflict in the present, and the emancipatory potential of the past, and of the folktale too, as expressed for instance by William Morris in his romances, *News from Nowhere*, *A Dream of John Ball*, and *The Sundering Flood*; and the deflection of revolutionary impulse was perhaps its primary purpose. And one can see the attractions: the largely middle

180 Barczewski, *op. cit.*, p. 106.
181 MacCarthy, F. (1994). *William Morris: A Life for Our Time*. London, Faber and Faber.
182 See MacCarthy, F. (2011). *The Last Pre-Raphaelite: Edward Burne Jones and the Victorian Imagination*. London.
183 Hill, *op. cit.*, Plate 52.
184 Thomas, S. K. (1983). *The Perception of the Past in Early Modern England*. London. Weidenfech and Nickolson.

THE USES OF THE PAST

class revivals of folklore, folkdance and song provided an illusory sense of continuity which has since become the hallmark of official British culture. This eventually set a global trend, and all over the world nations began to construct new identities by imagining themselves as old.[185]

Radical change of the kind experienced in Britain and especially Cornwall during the nineteenth century inevitably causes psychological and cultural dislocation. And this of course is much worse when minority cultures are being coerced in the interests of "national unity". New orthodoxies require the recording of the past which is thus reinvented over time, and is never merely "real". But a memory distorted in this way can no longer serve as a mirror to show us who we really are. Such strategies are perhaps rarely cynical in origin and are mainly unconsciously determined, though they may be and transparently often are shaped by self-interest. The problem was one of deep ambivalence, the huge creativity and energy of the Victorian period which brought with it an equally huge destructiveness.

---

185 See Anderson, B. (1982). *Imagined Communities: Reflections on the Origin and Spread of Nationalism*. London, Verso.

Chapter 5

Exile in Fiction

The most tragic loss experienced by Cornwall was the loss of its people. Mass emigration started around 1850 as the quality of copper ore deteriorated and other countries, particularly Chile, Australia and the United States increased their own output. Wages fell and in October 1863 the *West Briton* reported that:

> Large numbers of the mining population are emigrating to Australia, Chile, California, New Zealand, Queensland and the United States, but few bend their way to our Canadian possessions. This migration from St Just in Penwith, Camborne, St Agnes and St Blazey districts is becoming a matter of grave consideration, and mine agents and others are beginning to feel the scarcity of labouring hands—more especially when it is remembered that those who go abroad are the very bone and sinew of the country.[186]

The emotional consequences of all this can only be imagined, though as Lesley Trotter has said:

> Memories of women in nineteenth century Cornwall struggling to bring up families alone while their husbands were working abroad permeate the family histories of the Cornish all over the world, becoming part of the generalised folklore of the Cornish emigration.[187]

---

186 Barton, R. M. (1972). *Life in Cornwall in the Late Nineteenth Century*. Truro, D. R. Barton, p. 111.
187 Trotter, L. (2012). "Husband Abroad". In Payton, P. (ed) (2012). *Cornish Studies 20*, p. 196.

The pain of these thousands of simple people is largely unrecorded, and is deeper than history.

From ports such as Hayle hundreds of men took ship to Bristol and Liverpool and hence for Michigan or the Australian fields. As the crisis worsened Wheal Abraham, Wentworth Consols and many other western mines closed, and the financial crisis of 1866 produced a more widespread collapse. Thousands of families were plunged into near starvation and thousands more sought work overseas. Halliday tells us that:

> While the population of England and Wales grew steadily at the rate of thirteen per cent every ten years, that of Cornwall fell two per cent in the sixties, and a further nine per cent in the seventies, when a third of the mining population left the country.[188]

Out of such a small population this was a massive loss, and few families in the mining districts can have been unaffected by it.

Exile is a powerful and permanent experience. The Irish in Britain retain ancestral memories of the cattle boats and Americans by the million make the pilgrimage to Ellis Island to see where their ancestors landed, among those huddled masses yearning to breathe free. In Canada too Camerons and Farquarsons, Mackays and Mackenzies come together in their clan societies to share their identity, and, no doubt, a decent malt. Exile is permanent because, even if you revisit your former home, it is not the place you left: still less is it the fantasy world which emigrants often construct to comfort themselves for the loss of the real thing. *The Quiet Man*, the archetypal 1952 film of the emigrant's return, and its many successors, are fables to ease the pain of exile, not solutions: the past is not static; exiles inevitably recreate it to meet the needs of the present, not to mirror the reality of the past, which was grim. The result is an idealization. If "Innisfree" in the film was really as it appears in *The Quiet Man*, who could leave it? Who could possibly turn his back on Maureen

188 Halliday, *op. cit.*

O'Hara? (O'Hara used to chat with director John Ford in Irish during filming on location.)[189]

Cornwall in Fiction
The past of course can also or simultaneously be repackaged for the wider market as in Winston Graham's romantic "Poldark" novels and the television series which derive from them. Poldark's popularity gained a place for Cornwall in the wider British culture, and Alan Kent has expressed the view that:

> Within Poldark, heroism and romance under Cornish conditions were made plausible and admirable.[190]

which is more than could be said for most of the romantic fiction in which Cornwall forms the backdrop. And such fiction has a long history.

Alan Kent also defines the Anglo-Cornish literature of the late nineteenth century as characterized by "cultural introspection", often expressed in the form of "pulp Methodism" for a mass audience. The most successful practitioners of this kind of novel were the Hocking brothers, Silas and Joseph, and their sister Salome Hocking Fifeld. Silas and Joseph wrote a couple of hundred novels between them from the 1870s up to the 1930s. They are somewhat formulaic and rooted in the sentimental school of the mid-century, though they also depict Cornwall's later economic crisis quite effectively and make skilful use of the local background. Sometimes they are marred by a prescriptive form of Methodism which seems opposed to traditional Cornish culture, but at their best they are vivid and atmospheric, and they were evidently popular for many years. Among the best are Silas's *Sea Waif, Tregeagle's Head: A Romance of the Cornish Cliffs* and *Tales of a Tin Mine*; and Joseph's *The Birthright* of 1897, which describes John Wesley's mission to Cornwall in the eighteenth century. At their worst the Hockings were guilty of paranoid ranting against the Roman Catholic Church, in Joseph's

189 See *The Quiet Man* (1952), and McNee, G. (1990). *In the Footsteps of The Quiet Man*. Dublin, Mainstream.
190 Kent, *op. cit.*, p. 247.

"The Woman of Babylon", for instance, and "The Jesuit", this last an extraordinary story of a Jesuit plot to take over the British monarchy—in 1911! For the Hockings' Methodism formed the basis for a progressive, industrial Cornwall, carefully distinguished from its backward, superstitious Catholic past. While this may have provided some comfort and stability during the economic crisis it was inevitably exclusive and divisive. It also cut Cornwall off from its pre-Wesleyan past, that is from most of its history, and from the wider world: a new national identity could not be constructed on that basis. At the same time the romantic legacy has proved a heavy burden to later novelists, such as Daphne de Maurier, whose branch of historical fiction emphasized Cornish bleakness and harshness.[191] We have had to wait to our own time to find fiction which genuinely reflects the Cornish experience.[192]

Insofar as they are idealizations the reconstruction of the exile and the construction of place to meet the needs of the wider culture may resemble one another. The romantic film *The Quiet Man* was actually based on *Green Rushes*, Maurice Walsh's rather grim tale of wartime Ireland, though the film does not mention the war. It begins with the mother's voiceover: "And do you remember, Seánín, and how it was...", but in fact forgets more than it remembers. There is also "the myth of return" to this beautifully imagined place. The old country is not a museum (though in Cornwall as elsewhere much effort goes into trying to turn it into one), and even if it were it would not be the same to you, because you have changed and would not see it with the same eyes. When you are fifty and meet by chance the boy or girl you loved when you were eighteen, the result is not always unalloyed delight.

To a considerable extent the emigrant's view of both old and new countries will be shaped by the circumstances in which he or she left. The Cornish miners of the sixties would no doubt have preferred to stay at home, but their feelings would have been different from those of Irish Nationalists such as John Mitchell who were transported

---

191 Hughes, K. (1997). "A Silent, Desolate Country: Images of Cornwall in Daphne du Maurier's 'Jamaica Inn'." In Westland, *op. cit.*

192 In, for instance, Alan Kent's *Clay*, *Proper Job, Charlie Curnow!*, and *Voog's Ocean*, and N. R. Phillips' *Horn of Strangers* and *The Saffron Eaters*.

forcibly for their political views. A (relatively) free choice to make a new life across the ocean is obviously less traumatic than a forced departure due to famine or dispossession, though in practice there might not be very much difference. Apart from the basic task of earning a living and feeding and housing your family, or sending money home to them, a pressing psychological challenge was to maintain your personal and cultural identity in a setting which could be uncomprehending, indifferent or hostile. This required an ability to adapt to circumstances, to preserve what can be preserved, and to surrender what cannot. In order to do this emigrants often recreate their home communities and maintain customs which can lead to being scapegoated by their new neighbours. Old ways may seem irrelevant in a new country, and are often abandoned in the next generation. Cultural survival sometimes comes down to small things. The "Cousin Jacks" or more often one suspects "Cousin Jennies" of Michigan's Upper Peninsula, descended from Cornish miners, still take pride in their pasties. For those interested, they are filled with a basic mixture of meat, potatoes, onions, rutabagas (turnip) and carrots, and debate continues about the proper way to make them, which still has cultural significance in Michigan.[193]

Many things were lost though on the dangerous journey across the ocean. Traditional societies were bound together by family and religion, by customs which sanctified the commonplace, the shifting of the seasons and of human life, birth, coming of age, love and death. Nothing was too ordinary to be holy. Alexander Carmichael's *Carmina Gadelica*, a great collection of prayers gathered in the Scottish Highlands, included blessings for kindling and the smooring of the hearth, prayers for journeys and for the new moon, lullabies, invocations for waulking and for healing.[194] Robert Hunt has recorded the more fragmented system of belief and ritual which shaped life in nineteenth century Cornwall: he records cures for common ailments, ways to interpret the behaviour of birds and the

193 Lockwood, Y. R. and Lockwood, G. (1991). "Pasties in Michigan's Upper Peninsula: Food Ways, Inter-Ethnic Relations and Regionalism." In Stern, S. T. and Cicaca, J. (1992). *Creative Ethnicity*. Utah State University Press.
194 Carmichael, A. (1992). *Carmina Gadelica*. Edinburgh, Floris Books.

elements, and so on, most of which would have been impossible to transfer from the Lizard to South Australia.

Wherever they are, emigrants devise strategies to maintain their identities. Expatriate newspapers still illustrate some of these in the shape of social events, music and so on. Often these activities help to support threatened identities, for it is when we come together to share memories that we remember who we are, but this is difficult to sustain over the long term. The internet can help to create informal communities grouped around language, community or worship, but whether these will be strong enough to resist the hegemony of mass culture remains to be seen.

The Return in Fiction
Emigration and return were popular themes in nineteenth century fiction. Amy Clarke's *Roskelly of Roskelly* for instance, published in 1900, begins with the return of the heroine Meg to her grandmother's idyllic Cornish cottage, having finished her teaching job in England. Amy Clarke, who wrote under the name of Mrs Henry Clarke, was a popular writer of adventure stories, born in 1855 of Cornish parents, she died in 1908.[195] Her output was extensive like that of many Victorian novelists but she still found time to raise a family, read mathematics at Newham and become headmistress of Truro High School. Much of her historical fiction was set in Cornwall, which she knew and loved, and her descriptions still have an appealing freshness. She often write for young people, and her books made popular Sunday school prizes.

In *Roskelly of Roskelly* the plot centres on dissention in an old Cornish family as an old man commits a crime to regain his ancestral home, the "Roskelly" of the title. In the end this home has to be sold, and nothing is left of the fortune Roskelly has worked and sinned for, though an innocent member of the younger generation will inherit the name and the house. The theme of legitimate ownership of the land often recurs in Cornish culture: Arthur as "true king", the false king Teudar in the medieval plays, and in Joseph Hocking's

195 Clarke, Mrs H. (1900). *Roskelly of Roskelly*. London, SPCK.

The Birthright, subtitled *How he was robbed of his Birthright and how he tried to regain it.*[196]

As Meg returns we are told that "her father had been killed in the mine, and her mother had died of grief three months afterwards". We are also told of old Roskelly's return to his ancestral home, which his family had lost in a previous generation, establishing familiar themes of loss and appropriation. But with a moral the Hockings would have approved, loss can only be righted by virtue and Roskelly's criminality carries its own punishment: he acquired money on a sea voyage in some unexplained way and returned to Cornwall to claim his inheritance. Meg returns also to teach at the village school, and in the end she marries young Tom Roskelly. Alice Roskelly who has offended her father by marrying beneath her is reconciled with him shortly before his death.

Though the story is realistically told there are elements of the idealization and romanticism which the late Victorian reader had come to expect, corresponding with the new image of Cornwall as a tourist destination. On Meg's return, for instance:

> She had been away from Cornwall for years and this was her first sight of her old home. She had forgotten how beautiful it all was, she said to herself, as she drew deep breaths of delight.[197]

But when she eventually meets her aunt, this ideal picture is immediately shadowed by loss:

> "But you don't remember either of 'em—mother or feyther—do 'ee? You couldn't ha been above three year old when you lost 'em."[198]

Although old Roskelly has succeeded in making a lady of his daughter Susan, he doesn't really like her ladylike modern ways: in the matter of his old tobacco jar, for instance:

---

196 Hocking, J. (1897). *The Birthright*. London, Ward Locke.
197 Clarke, *op. cit.*, p. 6.
198 Clarke, *op. cit.*, p. 8.

Susie had once smuggled it away and replaced it by a gaily painted one which she bought for him in Folkestone. But he had insisted on having the old jar back; he could not enjoy his pipe unless he filled it from that. Though he had turned his back on his old life there were invisible threads binding him to it still.[199]

This defines the Cornish dilemma quite well, the tension between modernity and tradition. Though Roskelly has chosen his new road, like John of Chyanhor he secretly prefers the old one. This tension permeates the book along with issues of social change and class. Although Roskelly aspires to wealth and status his personal taste is for the comfortable old ways:

Dinner was the mid-day meal at Roskelly House unless there was company. Susie had made a good many attempts to get her father to dine late, but so far she had not been successful. He liked to take his ease when he came home and smoke hhis pipe with an old coat on. And he liked his dinner at the hour he had had it all his life.[200]

But for all that "he felt ill at ease there" because he did not really belong and had achieved his position by wrongful means.

Roskelly House itself is at the centre of the novel:

The most interesting part of it was the old kitchen with its vaulted stone roof and mighty hearth. It was much older than the rest of the house, being part of an older house which had been pulled down and rebuilt in the reign of James I. The date 1405 was rudely cut above the low-arched doorway. "We don't use it for a kitchen," Susie explained. "The servants would all give notice if we did. But they had a supper party here at Christmas and Miss Wyatt uses it sometimes for the meetings of her girls' club. I want to have an old folks' party after Easter."[201]

---

199 Clarke, *op. cit.*, pp. 28-9.
200 Clarke, *op. cit.*, p. 43.
201 Clarke, *op. cit.*, p. 62.

It is within this communal space, symbolic of Cornish heritage and values, that the pivotal event of the story takes place.

Earlier an old sailor named Pendennick returns to Roskelly after many years, in another homecoming reflecting Meg's return at the beginning, but with dramatic consequences. Pendennick had been a shipmate of Roskelly, and had witnessed him stealing the jewel which founded his fortunes and abandoning his companions to death, though he subsequently lost his memory of these incidents.

Susie plans her old folks' supper, and tries to persuade her brother Tom to tell the old people one of his adventures:

> "We are going to sit around the hearth and tell stories just as they used to do in the old times."[202]

But Tom advises her to:

> "Get the old people to tell their own stories. They will enjoy it much more than listening."

Susie replies, then says to her father:

> "But I don't want village talk. I wish poor old Pendennick had not lost his memory. I am sure he has had a very adventurous life. Papa, is it true that you have bought those cottages at the cove?"
>
> Mr Roskelly's brow darkened. "Yes, I am going to pull them down," he said briefly. Susie gave a little cry of dismay:
>
> "Oh papa, what will become of the people?"
>
> "I shall build better ones."[203]

Of course, at a time when social barriers were eroding, anxiety about social status was commonplace and was often depicted in the fiction of the time (in the work of Dickens and Mrs Braddon, for

---

202 *Ibid.*, p. 91. The scene recalls the setting of Bottrell's "Traditions and Hearth-side Stories of West Cornwall".

203 *Ibid.*, pp. 91-2.

instance), but this insistence on the importance of storytelling and shared memory is distinctly Cornish, and underpins both the medieval drama and the drolltelling tradition recorded by Hunt and Bottrell.[204]

This last dialogue is full of irony. Old Roskelly is trying to get rid of Pendennick, who lives in one of the cottages, to prevent the exposure of his crime, and so is pulled out of his normal position of supporting tradition. This in turn pushes Susie, a young lady who usually stands for smart modern ways, to support the dispossessed cottagers. The old and the poor, the repository of the community's storytelling tradition are to be brought together to share the stories which define their identity in this quintessentially Cornish place. ("They will enjoy it much more than listening.") But there are also less obvious ironies at work. "Poor Pendennick" does tell the story of "his very adventurous life", thereby exposing Roskelly's crime, and invalidating his claim to the ancestral home, and so Roskelly's threat to pull down the cottages and make Pendennick homeless in fact anticipates his own dispossession. The buildings we live in connect us with the past and inform our identities which is why Roskelly House means so much to Roskelly (the identity of names is significant). But by committing a crime he is false to himself and the values of his community. His crime is committed in the name of restoring his place in the community, but it leads to the planned destruction of the community itself, in order to get rid of Pendennick and protect his guilty secret.

Meg's Aunt Nance describes the scene in the old kitchen thus:

> "Miss Susie had a big cheer put for her feyther, and she went and fetched en in. He didn't half like it, I could see that. But Miss Susie, her'd got some maggot in her head about old times..."[205]

Tom tells a story after all:

---

204 I am not, of course, suggesting that Mrs Clarke borrowed from either.
205 *Ibid.*, p. 98.

"An then Margaret was asked to sing a song. Her's got a voice like a morning lark, the deer cheeld. Mr Pendennick was sitting just opposite her, next Mr Tom, and I seed en starin' at her, lookin' mighty strange. I couldn't keep my eyes off 'en. An when he'd come to an end, he got straight up from his cheer, holden on to the back of it with hiss two hands. 'It's come back, it's come back,' he screeched out. 'Twas the *Coromandel*. I was boatswain on her. An 'twas on a Friday us took to the boats."[206]

After a short pause in the narrative, Tom goes on to repeat Pendennick's story of his adventure on the desert island, where Roskelly had stranded them. Some months passed without Pendennick and his comrades sighting a ship until eventually Pendennick escaped. Roskelly had appropriated a sacred stone from a native temple (a fictional example of colonial looting) and escaped on a passing ship, without telling the captain about his companions, who were enslaved by the enraged islanders. Pendennick however, concludes by saying that he cannot remember the name of the friend who deserted him.

Roskelly is standing at the back of the room as the story is told, and though he manages to keep his secret he is transformed by the knowledge of what he is:

Mr Roskelly's secret died with him, and no shadow from it was left to darken his children's lives. But his ruin was complete. Roskelly had to be sold... Nothing was left of the fortune he had toiled and sinned for.[207]

The ending is ambivalent, so the family line may continue: one feels that the Hockings would have preferred a clearer judgement. But Pendennick's memory is at least partially restored by his return to his community and the telling of stories in a setting that recalls Hunt's storytelling sessions of a few generations earlier, and he can

206 *Ibid.*, p. 98.
207 *Ibid.*, p. 158. Roskelly's anxiety about exposure recalls that of Bulstrode in *Middlemarch*.

see his face in the mirror again, though Roskelly can no longer bear the sight of his own reflection as he is forced to remember what he has done, and that is his real punishment. He no longer lives in the home he desired so much, and for which he was prepared to dispossess others, but hope is invested in the coming generation, and the story ends on a note of hope because:

> There is a little lad at Hayle with Tom's square brow and Meg's blue eyes to whom he intends to leave it (the house), and who will one day be Roskelly of Roskelly.[208]

And the life of the community continues.

Though entertaining enough *Roskelly of Roskelly* is not a great novel, nor did Amy Clarke consciously set out to explore Cornish culture in any profound way. Nonetheless popular fiction often tells us more about its time than the more serious productions of self-consciously literary writers, if only because it needs to voice the preoccupations of its readers on a subconscious level in order to sell books. Walter Benjamin speaks of the "epic remembrance" which informs the novel and which derives from the oral tradition.[209]

208 *Ibid.*, p. 159.
209 Benjamin, W. (1999). *Illuminations*. London, Pimlico, p. 97.

Chapter 6

Voyages and Visitors

The Flying Indians

Amy Clarke was not of course the first novelist to write about Cornwall. *Peter Wilkins and the Flying Indians* or *The Life and Adventures of Peter Wilkins* by Robert Paltock was first published in 1751.[210] It is not set in Cornwall but tells the story of "a Cornishman". Paltock himself (1697–1767) was of Cornish parentage, though he was trained as an attorney and lived at Clement's Inn. His book is the story of a shipwrecked sailor in the style of Robinson Crusoe, but in a more fantastic vein. When marooned in Antarctica Wilkins encounters a nation of flying "Indians" (sic), one of whom, Youwarkee, he eventually marries. Wilkins introduces the Indians to technological innovation, but also aimed "at what we call civilising of them".[211] Very much the European of his time we see him gradually mastering his environment and then the people around him, converting them to his own code of self-reliance, hard work and Protestant Christianity.

> Pay your adoration to the Supreme Father of Spirits only, and to no wooden, stone or earthern deity whatsoever.[212]

This is very much of its time, complacent, rational, enlightened.

The story still entertains, and perhaps one should not examine it too closely for hidden meaning, but it does represent a trend in the English fiction of the time to explore encounters with other cultures, inspired by the voyages of British explorers.[213] In Gulliver's Travels,

---

210 Paltock, R. (1913 reprint). *The Life and Adventures of Peter Wilkins.* London, J. M. Dent.
211 *Ibid.*, p. 196.
212 *Ibid.*, p. 251.
213. See for instance Cook, J. (1999). *The Journals.* London, Penguin. Though the

Swift had already used this theme to satirize folly and corruption at home, and in 1719 Defoe published *The Life and Strange and Surprising Adventures of Robinson Crusoe* based on the adventures of Alexander Selkirk, a real life stranded mariner. This story of rugged Protestant individualism caught the mood of the time and inspired other works, including *Swiss Family Robinson*, *The Adventures of Philip Quarll*, and *Peter Wilkins* itself. Though often adapted for children, these books did explore the issues associated with colonialism, though with varying degrees of insight. *Peter Wilkins* is a relatively humane example, and its themes of exile and appropriation are certainly appropriate to Cornwall, though we are not of course invited to identify with the "Indians".

Money and Tin

Much closer to home and to the industrial modern world is Edward Bosanketh's novel *Tin*, based on real events in west Cornwall in the 1880s.[214] The story concerns the disappearance of a banker, and it seems to have caused a certain amount of bad feeling when it was first published locally because of its exposure of fraud in the mining industry. It has been described by Alan Kent as "the finest example of an indigenous Cornish novel of the nineteenth century": it is "a sophisticated expression of the complexity of nineteenth century Cornwall",[215] which at the same time analyses and criticizes the way in which industry actually works, and it is to that extent a subversive text. But it is ambivalent about the Cornish past.

> The people of west Cornwall differ in many material respects from those in the eastern part of the county. They are hardier, handsomer, and speak a different dialect. They are all that remain to us in this country of the original dark Celts who, by the force of numbers and the weapons of a more forward civilization, have been gradually pushed into one corner of the land. But the Celt is revenging himself on his conquerors, whenever he leaves his some and settles amongst

first account was written by John Hawkesworth and published in 1883.

214 Bosanketh, E. (1988 reprint). *Tin*. Marazion, Justin Brooke.

215 Kent, A., *op. cit.*, pp. 135-6.

the slower-witted Saxons, he invariably shows his superiority and comes to the front.[216]

It would seem from this that the sense of Cornish identity was still strong, at least in the west, and the fantasy of "revenge" upon the "conquerors" may also have been widespread, though it is expressed ambivalently here: the moral victory is the last resort of the defeated.

Armorel of Lyonesse

Sir Walter Besant published his *Armorel of Lyonesse* in 1890. It was popular at the time and is still in print. Besant was a social critic who wrote best-selling fiction. *Amorel* is partially set on Samson in the Isles of Scilly, though the scene later shifts to London. Besant was very much involved in the public life of his time and was a friend of Charles Dickens and Wilkie Collins: he completed the latter's unfinished novel *Blind Love*.[217] The "Lyonesse" of his title refers of course to the legendary sunken land to the west of Cornwall of which the Scillies are the surviving fragments, from an English point of view the land beyond the land beyond, and fishermen tell tales of muffled bells and a lost city. Similar stories are told of Mont St Michel, and another lost Cornish city is said to exist at Langarrow.[218] In medieval legend Tristan was a prince of Lyonesse.

So Besant's story is clearly placed in a legendary context. And Armorel herself, though described as a simple country girl, has the air and the name of a princess. (The novel is subtitled *A Romance of Today* and Samson described as "the enchanted island".) Armorel's life is interrupted by the arrival of a young English artist. Alan Kent points out that:

> This disruption from outside is a theme of most Celtic literatures: the disruption coming from the dominant neigh-bouring culture.[219]

---

216 *Op. cit.*, p. 107.
217 Clarke, W. (1988). *The Secret Life of Wilkie Collins*. London, Allison and Busby.
218 Deane, T. and Shaw (2003). *Folklore of Cornwall*. Stroud, Tempus, pp. 125-7.
219 Kent, *op. cit.*, p. 139.

The artist Roland Lee is attracted to Armorel and introduces her to the modern, outside world. But the legendary nature of the place and of the girl herself reasserts themselves. The pair visit an ancient barrow:

> Armorel looked into the grave. "They found," she whispered "the bones of the king lying on the stone. But when someone touched them they turned to dust. There is the dust at your feet in the grave. The wind cannot bear it away. It may blow the sand and earth into it, but the dust remains. The rain can turn it into mud, but it cannot melt it. This is the dust of a king."[220]

Lee rummaged around in the dust.

> Then he found something and drew it out and arose with the triumph that belongs to an archaeologist who picks up an ancient thing... it was of gold, a hoop of gold as thick as a lady's little finger, twisted spirally, bent into the form of a circle, the two ends not joined, but turned back. Pure gold, yellow, soft gold.[221]

It is of course a torque and after a brief dispute over ownership he gives it to Armorel "because you are the Princess of the Island". In the context of their developing relationship the image suggests that Lee has unearthed his own ancient Celtic princess, but it also, like the earlier passage, evokes the language of archaeology, in some ways the definitive nineteenth century science, and specifically perhaps the work of Schliemann, the famous discoverer of Troy.

Digging up the Past

In its early days archaeology was little better than looting. In a romantically restless spirit the gentleman-antiquaries plundered ancient sites for attractive artefacts to fill their cabinets and impress their friends. In the field William Stukeley (1687-1751) was the first

220 *Op. cit.*, p 27.
221 *Ibid.*, p. 28.

to attempt systematic study. But archaeology was not really possible until much later when the Danish scholar C. J. Thomsen published his *Guide to Northern Antiquities* in 1848, introducing the famous "three-age system", (that is, Stone Age, Bronze Age, Iron Age) still in common use today. From now on the appropriation of the past could proceed along orderly lines. Like other sciences archaeology was influenced by evolutionary thought, in its understanding of social development and the typology of artefacts for instance, and gradually the understanding of historical process became both possible and desirable.[222] There are other parallels which make archaeology an apt metaphor for Victorian England. Epistomophilia in the arts and sciences mirrors overseas expansion, and the acquisition of natural resources, such as Cornish copper and tin. As territorial acquisitions expanded overseas so intellectual hegemony expanded at home, and often the two went together: one thinks of the great excavations at Sumer and elsewhere in the Near East, in Egypt and the Indus Valley, in South America and perhaps particularly of Schliemann's work at Mycenae and Troy, in which gold spectacularly emerged from the dust.[223] To plant your flag on the surface of the earth was not enough, you had to plunder its contents in imagery that recalls Besant's imagined scene above, and perhaps inspired it. Schliemann uncovered a large treasure at Troy in 1873 which he called "Priam's Treasure", and masses of jewellery from the shaft graves at Mycenae in 1876, including a mummy wearing a gold mask which he removed. Finding the remains of a human face beneath (which rapidly disappeared on exposure to the air) he telegraphed the King of Greece, saying "I have gazed upon the face of Agamemnon".[224]

The importance of this episode is not always grasped. Here Schliemann was appropriating Homer and his world, which was the basis of literary culture in the west. Homer inspired "almost extravagant" worship "among educated Victorians, and was the

222 Renfrew, C. and Rafen, P. (eds) (1991). *Archaeology: Theories, Methods and Practice.* London, Thames and Hudson, p. 27.

223 See Daniel, G. (1968). *The First Civilisations: The Archaeology of their Origins.* Southampton, Camelot Press. And Traill, D. (1995). *Schliemann of Troy: Treasure and Deceit.* London, Penguin.

224 It wasn't and he hadn't, but this legend is now a part of the modern archaeological myth.

centrepiece of a classical education, and the ethical code that went with it".[225] Through Schliemann they were able to make him truly their own, just as they were able to take possession of other dead languages and ancient stories, in Cornwall and elsewhere. The mindset is the same. The image of the torque links Armorel with ancient Celtic story. Torques have in fact been found in Cornwall, most strikingly at Morvah in a group of six, though these are probably of Irish origin.[226]

Armorel continues to show Lee around the islands and narrate its legends to him. The place is cast in a romantic light (though Armorel herself follows the thoroughly modern profession of flower farming) and Lee tutors her in the "language of society". (The use of the innocent outsider to expose the falsity and corruption of civilization is an ancient literary strategy.) Every night in the family cottage a "rite of memory" is enacted: Armorel plays old tunes on her violin and her old grandmother is roused from her stupor by memories of the past:

> "We shall dance tonight," she said, "on Blyher Green. My boy will be there. We shall dance together. John Tryeth from Samson will play his fiddle. We shall dance 'Prince Rupert's March', and 'Blue Petticoats', and 'Dissembling Love'. The Ensign from the Garrison is coming and the Deputy Commissary. They will drink my health. But they shall not have me for partner. My boy will be there—my own boy— the handsomest man on all the islands—though he is so black. That's the Spaniard in him... it's the Spanish blood."[227]

Amorel comments:

> "Yes; the playing seems to put life and heart into her. All the morning she dozes, or if she wakes she is not often able to

---

225 Which of course had very little to do with the ancient Greeks.
226 Hencken, H. O. (1932). *The Archaeology of Cornwall and Scilly*. London, Methuen, p. 92.
227 *Op. cit.*, p. 41. "The Spanish Blood" is historical fantasy, still sometimes heard in Cornwall. It does serve to emphasize the racial "otherness" of the Cornish.

talk; but in the evening when we sit around the fire just as they used to sit in the old days, without candles—because my people were poor and candles were dear—and when Chessun spins and I play—she revives and sits up and talks. As you have seen her."[228]

And once again identity is enacted in a rite of collective memory. Archaeology is also an act of collective memory, and it developed technical expertise and theoretical coherence over the course of the nineteenth century with improved chronological sequencing and the ability to classify and arrange pottery and other artefacts, thus providing new ways of thinking about the past. Archaeology became global and competitive as Germany, France and the US developed their own archaeologies, and excavation became another arena for competing imperial ambitions.[229]

In the book Lee returns to London, and Armorel eventually follows him, to pursue her self-education and because she is in love with him. In the meantime he has fallen into the clutches of Feilding, a fraud who appropriates other people's work and passes it off as his own. Armorel frees Lee from Feilding's grip, recalling him to himself by playing her fiddle as she had at home on Samson, and disgusted by the corruption of modern society, the couple return to Lyonesse. The novel which was one of Besant's most popular, ends in the old Scillonian kitchen:

"It was all—except for the Ancient Lady and the hooded chair—all exactly as Roland remembered it nearly six years before. Yet, as Armorel said, though outside there was the music of the waves and within the music of her violin—the music was set to other words and arranged for another key. Between himself of that time, and of the present, how great a gulf!"[230]

---

228 *Ibid.*, p. 42.
229 For a brilliant fictional recreation of this period see Unsworth, B. (2009). *Land of Marvels*. London, Hutchinson.
230 *Op. cit.*, p. 317.

Rambles Beyond Railways

In the summer of 1850 Walter Besant's friend, the novelist Wilkie
Collins went for a walking tour in Cornwall, like Roland Lee, with
his friend the artist Henry C. Branding: he wrote a charming book
about their adventures.[231] As Alan Kent points out Cornwall had a
long tradition of travel writing going back to Richard Carew's *Survey
of Cornwall* in 1602.[232] The number of Cornish travel books was
growing with the growth of tourism and one of the best of them,
C. A. Johns' *A Week at the Lizard*, had recently been published when
Wilkie Collins began his journey.[233] The light-hearted tone of
Rambles Beyond Railways anticipated that of Roland Lee's trip to the
Scillies, and was characteristic of the literature. These books played
an important part in the cultural construction of Cornwall as a
holiday destination.

Collins was twenty-six when he began his Cornish holiday, but he
already had some reason to feel justified in his choice of career. Son
of the celebrated portrait painter William he had spent his early
adolescence touring Italy with his parents. He returned to London
to study law and was called to the Bar in 1849, though he never
practised. In 1851 he met Dickens and shared his editorial duties on
"Household Words" and later "All the Year Round". The two
writers had a fruitful collaborative relationship which spanned many
years. Collins of course is famous for his great "sensation" novels of
the sixties, *The Moonstone* and *The Woman in White*, and to a lesser
extent *Armadale* and *No Name*, though his drama and social novels
were also popular. His appetite for life was prodigious, and he kept
two family establishments, an arrangement which seems to have
worked remarkably well. Though his later life was marred by illness,
an over-enthusiastic use of narcotics, and a deterioration in the
quality of his literary output, his work is still widely read and adapted
for the screen.[234]

231 Collins, Wilkie (1851, reprint 1982). *Rambles Beyond Railways: Notes in Cornwall
  Taken Afoot.* Redruth, Tamar Books.
232 For later examples see for instance J. Henry Harris' cheerful 1906 travelogue
  Cornish Saints and Sinners or G. E. Mitton's *Cornwall* (1915). A. C. Black, both
  nicely illustrated.
233 Johns, C. A. (1992 reprint). *A Week at the Lizard.* Felinfach, Llanerck.
234 See Clarke, W. (1990). *The Secret Life of Wilkie Collins.* Stroud, Sutton.

In 1850 he had already published one novel, *Antonina or The Fall of Rome*. Though now unreadable, this novel belonged to the then fashionable genre of historical fiction, in part fuelled by the new archaeological discoveries, of which Bulwer-Lytton's *The Last Days of Pompeii* was a fair example, and it had a reasonably good critical reception. Historical fiction was an effective way of controlling and appropriating the past to serve the interests of the present, though Collins' early work does not, to our eyes, give much indication of the talent which was to produce the notorious "novels of sensation" a decade later and exert such influence over both "serious" and popular literature.

Collins was clearly in ebullient mood when he set off for Cornwall with his friend, and *Rambles* is one of the most delightful travel books ever written, though we will not be concerned with most of it here. Collins was an acute and witty observer, and his account is full of life and humour. He didn't like Helston, for which perhaps he need not be blamed, but his description of Loo Pool could hardly be bettered. It might be argued that the impression made on him by the Cornish countryside awakened a sensitivity to natural surroundings which he was later to put to powerful effect in, for instance, the description of Cobb's Hole in *The Moonstone*.

Traces of it are to be found in *The Dead Secret* and *Basil*, the novels he was researching at the time, but it was in any case a distinctively Victorian sensibility. Industrialization had produced new tensions in English society, generating class conflict. Factories brought large numbers of people together, and the close relatedness and solidarity of small communities was gone. The need of capitalist enterprises to amass profit in order to compete with each other eroded the old sense of social solidarity and left people feeling isolated and helpless. The working class across Britain created new institutions of their own to address this, and this happened in Cornwall too, but these organizations did not at this stage express a distinctively Cornish identity.

The French Revolution and Chartist agitation, along with the regular outbreaks of rioting (not least in Cornwall), combined with the erosion of religious belief, aroused fears of (or desires for) social revolution which persisted throughout the century. In this context the Wordsworthian love of nature became a longing for the prelapsarian imagined world of beauty and harmony which preceded the Industrial Revolution when even Londoners had access to unspoilt countryside. Compensation for this lost idyll was provided by literature, art, Thomas Cook and the growing tourist industry, Both art and the countryside could provide escapes from the ugly and alienated "City of Dreadful Night" realized brilliantly in Dickens' late novels, a return to a lost world of spiritual values, and Cornwall, in *Armorel of Lyonnesse* for instance, was an important part of this cultural repertoire.

The most gripping passage in *Rambles Beyond Railways* though is Collins' account of his descent into Botallack Mine, which evokes Cornwall's geological and industrial past rather than a lost rural idyll:

> [W]e get up to look at the rock above us. We are able to stand upright in the position we now occupy; and flaring our candles hither and thither in the darkness, can see the bright, pure copper streaking the dark ceiling of the gallery in every direction. Lumps of ooze, of the most lustrous green colour, transverse by a natural network of thin, red veins of iron appear and there in large, irregular patches, over which water is dripping slowly and incessantly in certain places. This is the salt water percolating through invisible crannies in the rock. On stormy days it spurts out furiously in thin, continuous streams. Just over our heads we observe a wooden plug of the thickness of a man's leg: there is a hole here, and the plug is all that we have to keep out the sea.[235]

Collins and Branding walked from Looe across to Land's End and along the north coast to Tintagel with digressions along the route. One of the attractions of the ancient western land was clearly its "beyondness", the fact that it was, though not for long, outside the tightening noose of homogeneity which was already throttling England.[236] This was the context in which Collins first encountered the Cornish "creation of the world", *Gwreans an Bys*. His encounter

235 *Op. cit.*, pp. 109-10.
236 See Westland, *op. cit.*

of the play is a unique account of a cultured Englishman's contact with an important piece of Cornish literature a century and a half ago, from an objective point of view.

The *Creation* was almost certainly composed around the middle of the sixteenth century and later transcribed by William Jordan in 1611, that is, in Shakespeare's lifetime. It is a miracle play, possibly related to the earlier *Ordinalia*, and dealing with the story in Genesis.[237] Such plays were common throughout Britain and western Europe, and tended to emphasize the importance of penitence for sin, though the story of Enoch appears to be unique to the Cornish play.

The edition which Collins read was based on the English translation by John Keigwyn made in 1691, corrected and published by Davies Gilbert in 1827: there are later and better translations available now. Collins' account of the play, which of course he never saw acted is preceded by an amusing account of "the modern drama in Cornwall", a bucolic version of the popular melodrama of the time; and by a rather good description of Piran Round, one of the old "playing places" in which traditional Cornish drama had been staged. He gives a fair account of the structure and versification of the play by way of introduction: it is in five acts, written in octosyllabic rhyme and so on. The text is one hundred and eighty pages long, he notes, with the eye of a professional dramatist, which

> Would be thought a lengthy manner of developing a dramatic story in our days: but we must remember that the time embraced in the plot of the old playwright extends from the Creation to the Flood, and must be astonished and thankful that he has not been more diffuse.[238]

This is a generous tribute across the centuries from one dramatist to another.

The Creation of the World is a somewhat paradoxical work, the only Cornish text to survive from the first half of the seventeenth century, a modernization and extension of the *Origo Mundi* from the *Ordinalia*,

237 See Murdoch, *op. cit.*, pp. 75-98.
238 *Op. cit.*, pp. 131-2.

and thus an extension of the medieval tradition into the early modern world, perhaps even a self-conscious attempt to preserve the language and its literature, though the times were not propitious.[239] Centres of Cornish learning and culture such as Glasney College had been destroyed at the Dissolution and the tradition of religious drama in the Cornish language performed in the open air (and often on the sites of ancient settlement) was ended. Yet even in this context Jordan seems to be making a conscious attempt to modernize the language and ensure its continuance. The act of memory was also an affirmation of hope and faith in the future.

The play was first printed in 1827 in Davies Gilbert's edition, but Gilbert neither knew nor cared for Cornish. Whitley Stokes 1807 edition for the London Philological Society was more scholarly, even though he produced his version in the course of a voyage to India.[240] As Brian Murdoch concludes:

> That we have only half a work, however, is a sad and inexplicable irony, just as it remains an irony of a different sort that a work like this, written at the end of the whole tradition of biblical drama, should have been copied out in a modernised and somewhat inconsistently spelled Cornish, in the year in which as far as drama is concerned, Shakespeare was still writing, and which in theological terms saw the commanding and unifying publication for Britain as a whole of the English King James Bible.[241]

More than one tradition was coming to an end, and *Gwreans an Bys* too belongs to a literature of loss.

Past and Present

Collins of course was not aware of the cultural implications. In the main his tone is courteous with perhaps a hint of gentle mockery, the tone of one who, while not unsympathetic, considers his subject

239 Kent, *op. cit.*, pp. 72-4.
240 Jordan, W. (1985). Retallack. Hooper, E. G. (ed). *Gwreans an Bys or The Creation of the World*. Redruth, Dyllansow Truran.
241 Murdoch, *op. cit.*, p. 98.

hopelessly quaint and old fashioned, and this perspective prevents him from engaging with the play as a living work of art, for instance:

> The author's speeches are wonderfully viscal and long; even his worst characters have, for the most part, a temperate and logical way of uttering the most violent language, which must have been an excellent lesson to the roistering young gentlemen among the audiences of the times.

There speaks the confident voice of Victorian England, a people proud of its empire and its industrial achievements, convinced (and assured by the Darwinian model) of its own cultural pre-eminence both in the contemporary world and in relation to the past. Though Victorians fretted about the future and idealized the past, in the novels of Sir Walter Scott, Gothic architecture and later pre-Raphaelite painting for instance, their belief in progress went deep, along with belief in themselves as history's crowning achievement: so in individuals too a manic optimism is sometimes coupled with depression and self-doubt, even despair. This ambivalence produced a tendency to disparage the past, especially the Roman Catholic past which was often designated simply as "superstition", if not an actual force for evil in the modern world, as in some of the Hockings' novels. This was part of a cluster of domains including women, folklore, emotion (as distinct from reason), subject races speaking minority languages and so on, all of which shared low status and childlike attributes calling for at best contemptuous indulgence, at worst brutal oppression. The report of the Committee of the Ethnographic Survey of the United Kingdom described the Cornish people as:

> Very warm and kindly, quick-witted and keen. Their faults are characteristically Celtic: they are not very "straight" and are exceedingly suspicious, they fall out easily among themselves, but do not make up again easily: feuds go on from year to year, and last out lifetimes. They have a very curious habit of giving by preference, any reason for their action except the one that has really determined it. The Cornish

Celt is prolific and exceedingly prone to sexual irregularity.[242]

Such a view, or something like it, seems to underlie the popular "Cornish" TV drama *Doc Martin*. The Cornish are tricky, unstable and indisciplined by nature, not unlike women, of whom it may be said:

> The influence of the womb upon the stomach is very remarkable... it is supposed that the influence of the womb on the brain may account for the greater number of instances of madness found in females than in males.[243]

There is perhaps a mere hint of this in Collins' take, but it is much more pronounced in the writings of English travellers who lacked his generosity of spirit.

The title of his little book suggests this tension between past and present, history and progress. The railway revolutionized communications in Britain, simultaneously symbolizing and actualizing the forces of progress and rationalism which led away from the medieval past. The novelist W. M. Thackerey compared the coming of the railway to Noah's Flood, when the Father told Noah:

> rag henna fysten ke gwra
> gorthell a planckys playnyes
> hag vnna leas trigva
> rowmys ẏ a vythe henwys (2254-57)

> Therefore hasten, go, make
> a ship of planks planed,
> And in it many dwellings,
> Rooms they shall be named.[244]

242 Williams, D. R. (2007). *A Strange and Unquenchable Race*. Truro, Dyllansow Truran, p. 72.
243 Graham, T. J. (1845). *The Diseases of Females: A Treatise Illustrating their Symptoms, Causes, Varieties and Treatment*. London, Simpkin and Marshall.
244 Jordan, *op. cit.*

Indeed, for Thackerey the railway was precisely the dividing line between past and present, ancient and modern:

> It was only yesterday, but what a gulf between now and then! Then was the old world, stagecoaches, more or less swift, riding horses, pack horses, highwaymen, knights in armour, Norman invaders, Roman legions, Druids, Ancient Britons painted blue and so forth—all these belong to the old period. I will concede a halt in the midst of it, and allow that gunpowder and printing tended to modernise the world. But your railroad starts the new era, and we of a certain age belong to the new time and the old one.[245]

It is interesting that Thackerey locates the Cornish—"Ancient Britons painted blue, and so forth"—in the past also.

To "ramble beyond railways" as Wilkie Collins did is therefore to journey into the past, a past which like the language and folklore of Cornwall, could only dwindle and die before the irresistible tide of the new.

But contemporary English attitudes as we have seen were quite complex: while minority cultures were denigrated and even actively persecuted they were also romanticized and sentimentalized, from *Ossian* on.

MacPherson had many imitators, down to the "sword and sorcery" epics of our own time. But later in the century serious scholars were busy translating authentic literature (though a surprising quantity has still not been published to this day), and Gilbert's *Creacion* is one example of this, another being Charlotte Guest's edition of *The Mabinogion* in 1849. When Collins took his Cornish holiday O'Kearney, O'Grady and the rest were working on the six volumes of translations which were soon to be published as the "Translations of the Ossianic Society", an epochal event in the history of Celtic Studies, and J. F. Campbell of Islay was preparing his magnificent *Popular Tales of the West Highlands*.[246]

---

245 Houghton, *op. cit.*, p. 3.
246 Campbell (1983-84 reprint). *Popular Tales of the West Highlands*. Vols. I-IV. Edinburgh, Wildwood House.

VOYAGES AND VISITORS

It was becoming increasingly difficult to dismiss the traditional literatures of the Celtic nations as a crude and rustic curiosity as an ever-larger readership became aware of its real quality. MacKillop describes the 1850s as a turning point, the period in which the old amateur antiquarianism began to give way to real scholarship.[247] For this and for other reasons it was a time when English attitudes towards Celtic culture, at least among the cultured elite, were becoming more complex and uncertain. This in turn was part of a wider tendency to ambivalence, a result of differing emotional responses to profound social and economic change. Something of it may be recalled in the Celtic Library at Jesus College, where one is surrounded by magnificent books written and collected by the Victorians (the library was once the study of Sir John Rhys, the first Professor of Celtic Studies). When one considers that all this was done at a time when the communities which spoke these languages were being deliberately destroyed. It was comforting to think that this was part of the divine plan. As Herbert Spencer write, in the year *Rambles Beyond Railways* was published:

> The poverty of the incapable, the distress which come upon the imprudent, the starvation of the idle, and those shouldering aside of the weak by the strong, which leave so many 'in shallows and in miseries' are the decrees of a large, far-seeing benevolence.[248]

The violence of the age was of course huge, and its social causes were beginning to be understood. The potato blight attacked Ireland in 1845, and exacerbated by British Government policy a combination of starvation and emigration caused the population to fall from eight to five million.[249] In Cornwall rioting provoked by food shortages persisted throughout the century, and hunger also stimulated emigration. In the first six months of 1875, reported the West Briton:

247 See Mackillop, *op cit.*, Introduction.
248 Houghton, *op. cit.*, p. 209.
249 Curtis, E. (1901) *A History of Ireland*. London, Methuen.

Ten thousand five hundred and seventy-six emigrants left Cornwall for the Australian colonies... but there is no certain record of the number who have emigrated to Canada and to North and South America. It must be very large... Emigration is still going on, and would go faster were it not that so many who are left have no money to pay the passage.[250]

The immediate cause of this wave of emigration seems to have been the fall in the price of tin, but the food riots caused by the loss of the potato crop led to the active promotion of emigration as a "solution" to Cornwall's periodic crises.[251] In the meantime rioting was put down with a heavy hand, though not so heavy as to rival the brutalities perpetrated overseas by Governor Eyre of Jamaica for instance, or Rajah Brooke in Sarawak, to take only the more egregious examples.[252] There can be little doubt that Victorian sensibilities were coarsened by the Carlylean cult of force, the idea that might is right, reinforced by an explicitly racist ideology.

Wilkie Collins' discussion of the play continues. He is scathing about the fifth act:

which it would be doing the old author no kindness to examine... in detail, Here, he sinks again in many places to puerility of conception and coarseness of dialogue.

But though he feels entitled to criticize the medieval play for not coming up to the standard of contemporary drama, he is also clearly engaged with it as theatre, and in a fine passage vividly reconstructs the original performance, albeit in a slightly mocking style; the fight among the angels, the descent of the damned, Cain falling out of the bush as he is struck by Lamech's arrow. He is himself too much of a dramatist to be blind to the power of the play, yet too much an Englishman of his time quite to accept it on its own merits: the result is an account which captures exactly the ambiguity of the cultural moment.

---

250 Barton, R. M., *op. cit.*, pp. 367-70.
251 Deacon, B., *op. cit.*, p. 140.
252 Houghton, *op. cit.*, p. 212.

Yet in the end Collins' integrity impels him to make a value judgement, as he compares the tawdry melodrama he has seen at Redruth with his imaginative reconstruction of the *Creacion*:

> If we set them fairly against one another as we now know them, would it be rash to determine which burnt purest, the new light that flared brilliantly in our eyes when we last saw it, or the old light that just flickered in the socket for an instant, as we tried to trim it afresh? Or, if we rather enquire which audience had the advantage of witnessing the worthiest performance should we hesitate to decide at once? Between the people of Redruth and the people of Piran Round there was certainly a curious resemblance in one respect—they failed alike to discern the barbarisms and absurdities of the plays represented before them; but were they also equally uninstructed by what they beheld? Which was likeliest to send them away with something worth thinking of, and worth remembering, the drama about knaves and fools at the modern theatre, or the drama about scripture history at the ancient? Let the reader consider and determine.[253]

Joseph Pearce's "Drolls"

One of the most interesting late nineteenth century Cornish writers was Joseph Henry Pearce who was born in Penzance in 1856. In 1877 like so many young Cornish people before and since he moved to London where he worked as a clerk, devoting his leisure time to writing. His first book *Bernice*, a tragedy set in Cornwall, was published in 1890, and has been described as "one of the best Cornish stories ever penned".

In 1891 *Inconsequent Lives* was published, and two years later *Jaco Treloar*, another Cornish tale. Pearce's two collections of imaginative stories and fantasies entitled *Drolls from Shadowland* and *Tales of the Masque* appeared in 1893 and 1894 respectively: they were reprinted together in 1998 by Llanerch Press.[254] His later books included *Eli's*

253 *Op. cit.*, p. 140.
254 Pearce, J. H. (1998) (ed. C. D. Pollard). *Cornish Drolls*. Felinfach, Llanerch Press.

Daughter, Cornish Drolls and *The Dreamer's Book*, and though he is almost forgotten now Pearce seems to have enjoyed a moderate degree of popularity in his own time: favourable reviews survive, and several of his works went into further, including American editions. In the course of time he returned to his beloved Cornwall, spending his retirement at St Austell where he eventually died.

Pearce's lifetime was a period of unprecedented change in British society. In the last seventy years of the nineteenth century the population increased by ten per cent in each decade, becoming more concentrated and urbanized. Railways and industrialization transformed whole regions and combined with periodic agricultural depressions from the mid-seventies on sucked thousands of farm labourers and their families into the expanding towns and cities. Cornwall was at the forefront of these developments and was one of the first regions to industrialize, introducing deep mining and following the exploitation of copper with that of tin. Later in the century both industries went into crisis as international competition intensified, but arsenic and clay mining took their place, along with the engineering expertise for which the Cornish were justly famous.[255] Communications improved, but the clock was ticking for the Cornish economy faced as it was with increased competition, the constant need to import coal, and the perennial problem of its marginalization within Britain itself. Cornish farming was mainly of a subsistence nature, and the "Hungry Forties" and the economic crises that followed caused mass emigration to California, South Australia and South Africa particularly.

Although overall wealth increased over the period increasing numbers of people began to question its distribution, and slum housing, poverty and appalling working conditions became highly visible social evils. As the century wore on trade unions emerged and attempted to redress the balance between owners and workers, and in 1872 for instance, Cornwall saw mass strikes in an attempt to end the traditional, and notorious "five week month" in the mining industry.[256] A grim winter of industrial trench warfare ensued when

255 See Payton, P. (1992) *The Making of Modern Cornwall. Redruth.* Dyllansow Truran, Chapters 4 and 5.
256 Deacon, B., *op. cit.*, p. 154.

workers in the clay country struck to impose a closed shop, and employers responded with a lock-out.

The rise of socialism and union activism in Britain, though it provided hope for many, eroded the confidence of the property-owning class.

This was also a time of great spiritual and intellectual ferment. As early as 1833 Charles Lyell in his *Principles of Geology* had argued that the natural history of the planet could be satisfactorily explained in terms of the workings of natural forces alone, a position which seemed to leave little room for the God of tradition, and the publication of Darwin's *Origin of Species by Natural Selection* in 1859 seemed to many to confirm science as the enemy of faith. As the Bishop of Oxford wrote in *The Quarterly Review*:

Man's desired supremacy over the earth: man's power of articulate speech; man's gift of reason, man's free will and responsibility, man's fall and man's redemption... all are equally and utterly irreconcilable with the degrading notion of the brute origin of him who was created in the image of God, and redeemed by the eternal son assuming to himself his nature.

Charles Bradlaugh preached militant atheism to mass meetings of working men, and though his views were too extreme for most, he undoubtedly contributed to the national mood of unease, at a time when it was widely believed that religion was a necessary force for social cohesion and a defence against revolution, whether the people actually believed in it or not. Cornwall was a place where religion still mattered, but even there radical change was taking place. The Established Church was associated with the Tory English establishment, and had lost the confidence of many ordinary people. This left the Cornish with a deep spiritual hunger which John Wesley set out to fill. He visited Cornwall nearly thirty times in the course of half a century and his preaching was particularly popular in the densely populated mining districts of the far west.[257] The establishment responded with "a panicky persecution" that failed to stem the

257 See Halliday, *op. cit.*, pp. 266-7.

tide, and Methodism became a distinctively Cornish faith, setting it apart from the largely Anglican south of England, and it was often praised for its moral effects on the population. Wesley

> brought hope to hopeless thousands, and thanks largely to him the Cornwall of 1790 was a far less barbarous place than it had been in 1740. Drunkenness had declined, and though smuggling had never been so prosperous, the inhumanities of wrecking had been checked.[258]

But despite these undoubted gains Methodism disapproved of traditional Cornish "superstitions", and it was said of Uncle Anthony, the traditional singer, that

> He sang religious songs too, but avoided the Methodists who disapproved of his art.[259]

And this seems to have been a factor in the decline of traditional storytelling, due to what Hunt describes as:

> the constantly-repressing influences of Christian teaching and of the advances of civilisation.[260]

This argument may be overstated. Traditional Cornish culture co-existed with Christian teaching quite happily for many centuries.

Rapid change, even positive change, produces uncertainty and there can be little doubt that many clung to Methodism to provide a sense of safety in a rapidly-changing world. This sometimes led to a certain narrowness of outlook, an intolerance of difference (among the Bryanites or "Bible Christians" for instance who were often presented unfavourably in the popular fiction of the time).[261] But at last, after centuries of alienation and indifference, Cornwall had a religious narrative it could call its own.

---

258 *Ibid.*, p. 277.
259 Deane and Shaw, *op. cit.*, p. 217.
260 Hunt, *op. cit.*, p. 24.
261 In Arthur Quiller-Couch's *The Ship of Stars* (1899) for instance.

Spiritual uncertainty is certainly present in Pearce's stories, in which the innocent are as likely to suffer as the guilty, loss is ever-present and redemption problematic. Victorian pessimism found its fullest expression in James Thomson's masterpiece, *The City of Dreadful Night*, first published episodically in 1874 but subsequently reprinted many times, though little read today. This mood was a characteristic of wider British society, and a counterweight to the optimism and self confidence which also typified the period. Says Thomson's preacher:

> We bow down to the universal laws, which never had for
> man a special clause, of cruelty or kindness, love or hate.

And we meet the same sense of the indifference of a universe in which man no longer filled the centre in such "drolls" as "The Sorcery of the Forest" and "A Voyage to the Golden Land". Pearce expresses it most clearly in this verse from "Esther Dentreath":

> We only know there is one end for all,
> However we shape our lives:
> Beneath the mournful darkness of the fall
> No certain hope survives.

Not infrequently the mood is heightened by some bleak Cornish setting of moorland, mine or stormy sea, against which background a doomed protagonist acts out his or her allegorical conflict, rather as in Hardy, and the outcome is rarely comforting.

Brunel's bridge over the Tamar was completed in 1859 and in that year the first train ran from Plymouth to Truro. Wilkie Collins' book was only the first to tell the new story of Cornwall as a tourist destination and to inaugurate a new industry, indeed a new identity. And one can see why. The ancient Celtic land was remote yet accessible, British yet indefinably foreign, and had breathtaking coastal scenery despite the industrial squalor of the mining districts. Improved communications and integration with the rest of Britain began to dilute traditional folkways and facilitated emigration during the economic crisis and Joseph Pearce too was forced to leave home, though in his fiction he often returned home to the land of his birth. "Joanna" in the story of that name is the daughter of a "bal" or mine girl, and "The Man who Coined his Blood into Gold" is a Cornish tinner. In "Joel", "The Valley of Vanished Sunsets" and "A Pleasant Entertainment" he deals explicitly with themes of exile and loss, which surely had a strong personal resonance for him.[262]

Pearce's Cornish stories are noteworthy for their use of folklore motifs. Hunt's *Popular Romances* had appeared as a response to increased curiosity about Cornwall, and as he wrote in his preface to the 1881 edition:

> The railways give great facilities for visiting those scenes of which the public eagerly avail themselves. But they have robbed the West of England of half its interest by dispelling the spectres of romance which were, in hoar antiquity, the ruling spirits of the place.[263]

By a paradox which has become sadly familiar the erosion of an authentic tradition was accompanied by its cultural fossilization: much the same thing had already happened to the Cornish language. Pearce's own knowledge of Cornish folklore was clearly extensive, and was frequently tuned to allegorical ends, as in "The Man Who Met Hate". "The Haunted House" draws on "piskies, buccaboos and other folktales of the hamlet", and the children in that bleak tale "A Voyage to the Colden Land" make passing reference to the funerary rites of ancient Lyonesse. Moreover, folklore not infrequently provides narrative structure, in "Little Crow of Paradise" for instance and "The Man who had Seen". Pearce uses these motifs with a certain restraint employing these "spectres of romance" in the service of his own austere vision.

The use of folklore in the literature of the period was widespread. Science had become inextricably associated with "progress", a vague term which Darwin and Huxley themselves would certainly have questioned, and had in consequence become increasingly grandiose

262 Pearce, *op. cit.*
263 Hunt, *op. cit.*, p. 1.

in its claims. "Modern science", wrote Professor Pearson, one of its apologists, in 1892,

> does much more than demand that it shall be left in undisturbed possession of what the theologian and metaphysician please to term its legitimate field. It claims that the whole range of phenomena, mental as well as physical—the entire universe—is its field.

Faced with such overweening arrogance writers adopted a variety of strategies to defend imagination and the human spirit, and folklore, which embodied a vision of the individual and communal space in the natural order that was far older than the scientific paradigm, became, along with the supernatural, a weapon in their hands. Unfortunately, as with the tension between religion and science, a false dichotomy emerged between "true" progressive science and "false" regressive supernaturalism, which served neither. Some writers even invented new narrative forms which turned the laws of science on their heads, and in so doing they found ways of exploring human experience which began where science left off.[264]

English literature also changed considerably during Pearce's lifetime, in response to a changing economic and cultural climate. The growth of literacy following the 1870 Education Act and the need for a more literate workforce, the demise of the old three-volume novel and the rise of the short story, in part due to the rapid growth of literary periodicals in the nineties, contributed to the development of a literature which provided both an escape from and a symbolic expression of the conflicts and ambiguities of the time, taking on some of the functions of folklore and borrowing extensively from it.

The literature of fantasy and the supernatural had its roots in the Romantic movement, which was in turn a response to the rationalism of the Enlightenment. In the construction of their alternative realities, as we saw with *Ossian*, romantic writers drew on myth and legend belonging either to their own country's remote past or to more exotic traditions, which were becoming more widely

---

264 For example Lewis Carroll, George MacDonald, Lord Dunsany.

known thanks to foreign exploration and new translations of old texts. So Keats for example based his "Isabella" on a story from Boccaccio's *Decameron* and "La Belle Dame Sans Merci" on medieval chivalric tradition, while Tennyson later made use of Arthurian stories, some of them Cornish in origin, for his *Idylls of the King*.

By the 1890s a subversive literary tradition was already well established, and the short story give it a new lease of life. Some writers of course had a clearer sense of purpose than others and the development of different genres complicated the picture. William Morris for instance, some of whose fantasies drew upon the saga literature of medieval Iceland, was explicitly radical and taught an emancipatory message.[265] "Apart from the desire to produce beautiful things," he wrote in 1894, "the leading passion of my life has been and is hatred of modern civilisation"; and we find something of this spirit in some of Pearce's stories.

But in the end the complexity and variety of artistic response in the 1890s are too great to be even summarized. Undoubtedly many late Victorians were content, even complacent: there had, after all been no revolution in 1848, though it was a close-run thing. In spite of Chartism and the prophecies of Carlyle, and for many in the expanding middle-class the progress celebrated in the Diamond Jubilee of 1897 seemed a reality. But there were dissenting voices, such as the later Dickens, and the Trollope of *The Way we Live Now*, later attacks on the sanctity of family life and the role of *The Angel in the House*, by Gosse and Samuel Butler, the aestheticized socialist critique of Oscar Wilde and the romantic yearnings of Millais, Rossetti, and their Pre-Raphaelite followers, with their explicit rejection of the vulgar present.

Throughout the period though there was also a growing awareness of the dark side of the psyche. The first volume of *The Golden Bough*, with its encyclopaedic accounts of human irrationality and absurdity appeared in 1890, and Freud's *Studies on Hysteria* five years later, marking the first attempt to explore the contents of the unconscious mind. The last decades of the century witnessed the beginnings of psychiatry and psychology as distinct disciplines, much as

265 See for instance his *Sigurd the Volsung* (1878) and *The Wood Beyond the World*. And MacCarthy, F. (1994). *William Morris: A Life for our Time*.

missionaries, traders and explorers were uncovering the secrets of "the Dark Continent" and sending home accounts of their discoveries to a fascinated Victorian public, so a different kind of adventurer was beginning to map the jungles of the mind, and the results in both cases could be unsettling, and this was not without its echoes in literature: the inner and outer journeys came together in 1902 in Joseph Conrad's superb *Heart of Darkness*.

The Irishman Sheridan Le Fanu, perhaps the greatest teller of supernatural tales, reflects this introspective mood in his 1872 collection *In a Glass Darkly*: is the unfortunate clergyman in "Green Tea" for instance a victim of some evil external force, or is he suffering from some unresolved internal conflict, as Freud would have said. Le Fanu, as Bleuler has said, was interested in evil:

as a peculiar experience that can befall man, something that comes from outside yet is matched from inside.[266]

Many of his stories are based on folktales he heard from Miss Anna Baily of Lough Guir in Limerick, and he also assisted Samuel Carter Hall in his compilation of Irish folktales. This blurring of the boundaries between the internal and external worlds is also to be found in Pearce's stories, and one is never quite certain to what extent characters such as the Presence in "The Veil of May" or the pedlar in "The Comedy of a Soul" are meant to be taken literally, or how far they are intended to represent externalized psychological forces, or even allegorical figures in a morality play.

Pearce's stories cannot reasonably be compared with those of Le Fanu. The laconic, almost minimalist Cornish stories seem impoverished beside the richly textured tales of the Irishman. But taken on his own terms Pearce does succeed in catching something of the temper of his times, something of their ambivalence and disillusion, shading at times into despair. Where these wider moods appear to be informed by a deeply felt personal sadness which may also embody the Cornish experience, the result can be oddly moving.

266 See Bleuler's introduction to Le Fanu, J. S. (1975). *Ghost Stories and Mysteries*. New York, Dover.

Conclusion

The central theme of this book has been the importance of the act of shared memory in reconstituting identity in every generation, since without memory we cannot understand what we are. This is particularly so where the traditional culture of the community has been under threat from a powerful neighbour, as is the case in Cornwall, and this is why the pattern tends to recur, not because of any direct cultural transmission, but because the same problems evoke similar responses. These responses will also be influenced by forces in the wider culture, which is why so much of the book deals with the ideology of Victorian Britain. In such a setting storytelling becomes an act of cultural resistance.

Bibliography

Alcock, Leslie (1971). *Arthur's Britain*. London, Allen Lane.

Angarrack, John (1999). *Breaking the Chains*. Cambourne, Stannary Publications Passim.

Apuleius (trans. Robert Graves) (1950). *The Golden Ass*. Harmondsworth, Penguin.

Arnold, Matthew (1910) (1867). *On the Study of Celtic Literature and other Essays*. London, J. M. Dent.

Attwater, Donald (1965). *The Penguin Dictionary of Saints*.

Bakere, Jane (1980). *The Cornish Ordinalia: A Critical Study*. Cardiff, University of Wales Press.

Baldick, Chris (ed.) (1992). *The Oxford Book of Gothic Tales*. Oxford, Oxford University Press.

Barkan, David (1996). *The Duality of Human Existence: Isolation and Communion in Western Man*. New York, Beacon Press.

Barczewski, Stephanie L. (2000). *Myth and National Identity in Nineteenth Century Britain*. Oxford, Oxford University Press.

Berresford Ellis, Peter (1974). *The Cornish Language and its Literature*. London, Routledge and Kegan Paul.

Bettelheim, Bruno (1976). *The Uses of Enchantment: The Meaning and Importance of Fairy Tales*. New York, Alfred A Knopf. Reprint (1978), Harmondsworth, Penguin.

Birch, Lionel (1906). *Stanhope, A., Forbes A. R. A., and Elizabeth Stanhope Forbes, A. R. W. S.* London, Cassell.

Booker, Christopher (2004). *The Seven Basic Plots: Why we Tell Stories*. London, Blooksbury.

Bottrell, William (1870). *Traditions and Hearthside Stories of West Cornwall*. Penzance, the author. Reprint (1996), Lampeter, Llanerch Press.

Bottrell, William (1880). *Stories and Folklore of West Cornwall*. Reprinted (1996), Llanerch.

Bray, Anna Eliza (1844). *Traditions, Legends, Superstitions, and Sketches of Devonshire on the Borders of the Tamar*. 2 vols, London.

Breait, H. (1952). *400 Centuries of Cave Art Montignac*. Centre d'Études et de Documentation Pré-Historiques.

Briggs, Asa (1963). *Victorian Cities*. London, Odhams.

Briggs, Katherine (1967). *The Fairies in Tradition and Literature*. London, Routledge and Kegan Paul.

Briggs, Katherine (1976). *A Dictionary of Fairies*. London, Allen Lane.

Broome, Dora (1963). *Fairy Tales from the Isle of Man*. Douglas, Modern Press.

Campbell, John Francis (1860–61). *Popular Tales of the West Highlands*. 3 vols, Edinburgh, Edmonston and Douglas. Reprint (1983–84), Hounslow, Wildwood House.

Carew, Richard (1602). *Survey of Cornwall*. Reprinted (2000), Redruth, Tamar Books.

Chadorow, Nancy (1978). *The Reproduction of Mothering: Psychoanalysis and the Sociology of Gender*. Berkeley, University of California Press.

Collins, Wilkie (1851). *Rambles Beyond Railways*. London, Richard Bentley. Reprint (1982), London, A Mott.

Collins, Wilkie. *The Moonstone*.

Collins, Wilkie. *The Woman in White*.

Courtney, Margaret Ann (1886). *Cornish Feasts and Folklore*. Reprinted (1998), Oakmagic.

Crossing, William (1890). *Tales of the Dartmoor Pixies: Glimpses of Elfin Haunts and Antics*. London, Hood.

Curl, James Stevens (1990). *Victorian Architecture*. Newton Abbot, David and Charles.

Curtin, Jeremiah (1890). *Myths and Folklore of Ireland*. London, Sampson Low, Marston, Searle and Rivington. Reprint (1975), New York, Gramercy.

Davidson, Hilda Ellis and Anna Chaudhri (eds.) (2003). *A Companion to the Fairy Tale*. Cambridge, D. S. Brewer.

Deacon, Bernard, Dick Cole, and Garry Tregigda (2003). *Mebyon Kernow and Cornish Nationalism*. Cardiff, Welsh Academic Press.

Deacon, Bernard, (2007). *Cornwall: A Concise History*. Cardiff, University of Wales Press.

Deane, Tony, and Tony Shaw (1975). *The Folklore of Cornwall*. London, Batsford. Reprint (2003), Stroud, Tempus Publishing.

Desmond, Adrian, and James Moore (1991). *Darwin*. London, Michael Joseph.

Dorson, Richard M. (1968). *The British Folklorists*. London, Routledge and Kegan Paul.

Drabble, Margaret (ed) (2000). *Oxford Companion to English Literature*. Oxford, Oxford University Press.

Duffy, Maureen (1972). *The Erotic World of Faery*. London, Hodder and Stoughton.

Dundes, Alan (1984). *Sacred Narrative: Readings in the Theory of Myth*. University of California Press.

Enright, Michael J. (1996). *Lady with a Mead Cup: Ritual, Prophecy and Lordship in the European Warzone from La Tène to the Viking Age*. Dublin, 4 Courts Press Passim.

Evans, Eric J. (1983). *The Forging of the Modern State: Early Industrial Britain, 1783–1870*. London, Pearson.

BIBLIOGRAPHY

Everson, Michael, Craig Weatherhill, Ray Chubb, Bernard Deacon, and Nicholas Williams. (2007) *Form and Content in Revived Cornish: Articles in criticism of Kernowek Kemyn*. Cathair na Mart, Evertype.

Faber, Geoffrey C. (1933). *Oxford Apostles: A Character Study of the Oxford Movement*. London, Faber and Faber. Reprint (1954), Harmondsworth, Penguin Books.

Fletcher, Anthony (1968). *Tudor Rebellions*. London, Longmans.

Ford, Boris (ed) (1992). *Cambridge Cultural History of Britain. Volume 7: Victorian Britain*. Cambridge, Cambridge University Press.

Gay, Peter (1988). *Freud: A Life for our Time*. London, Dent.

Georges, Robert A., and Michael Owen Jones (1995). *Folkloristics: An Introduction*. Bloomington, Indiana University Press.

Gilbert Davies (1826) *Mount Calvary, Interpreted in the English Tongue*. London, Nichols.

Gimbutas, Marija (1989). *The Language of the Goddess*. London, Thames and Hudson.

Glasscock, Carl B. (1938). *The War of the Copper Kings*. New York.

Grant, Isabel F. (1961). *Highland Folk-Ways*. London, Routledge and Kegan Paul.

Green, Miranda (1986). *The Gods of the Celts*.

Grennan, Margaret Rose (1945). *William Morris, Medievalist and Revolutionary*. New York, King's Crown Press.

Griscom, Acton (ed) (1929). *Geoffrey of Monmouth, Historia Regum Britannia*. New York.

Hale, Amy, Alan M. Kent, and Tim Saunders (eds) (2000). *Inside Merlin's Cave: A Cornish Arthurian Reader 1000–2000 AD*.

Halliday, F. E. (1955). *The Legend of the Rood*. London, Duckworth.

Halliday, F. E. (1959). *A History of Cornwall*. London, Gerald Duckworth.

Hamilton Jenkin, Alfred Kenneth (1927). *The Cornish Miner*. London, Allen and Unwin.

Hamilton Jenkin, Alfred Kenneth (1933). *Cornwall and the Cornish: The Story, Religion and Folk-lore of the Western Land*. London, J. M. Dent.

Harte, Jeremy (2004). *Explore Fairy Traditions*. Loughborough, Heart of Albion.

Hartland, Edwin Sidney (1891). *The Science of Fairy Tales: An Inquiry into Fairy Mythology*. London, Walter Scott.

Heaney, Seamus (2010). *Beowulf: A Verse Translation*. London, Folio.

Hill, Charles Peter (1977). *British Economic and Social History 1700–1975*. London, Edward Arnold.

Hill, Rosemary (2007). *God's Architect: Pugin and the Building of Romantic Britain*. London, Allen Lane.

Hobsbawm, Eric (1962). *The Age of Revolution 1789–1848*. London, Weidenfeld and Nicolson.

Hobsbawm, Eric (1975). *The Age of Capital*. London, Weidenfeld and Nicolson

Hooper, E. G. Retallack (eds) (1985), *Gwryans an Bys or The Creation of the World*. Redruth, Dyllansow Truran.

Howells, William (1831). *Cambrian Superstitions*. London, Longmans. Reprint (1991), Felinfach, Llanerch Press.

Hughes, Winifred (1980). *The Maniac in the Cellar: Sensation Novels of the 1860s*. New Jersey, Princeton University Press.

Hull, Eleanor (1928). *Folklore of the British Isles*. London, Methuen.

Hunt, John Dixon (1982). *The Wider Sea: A Life of John Ruskin*. London, Dent.

Hunt, Robert (1881). *Popular Romances of the West of England*. London, Chatto and Windus.

James, Ronald M. (1992). "Knockers, knackers and ghosts. Immigrant folklore in the western mines". In *Western Folklore*, vol 51, Part 2, 153–177.

Jenkins, A. K. Hamilton (1927). *The Cornish Miner*. London, Allen and Unwin.

Jenkins, A. K. Hamilton (1933). *Cornwall and the Cornish*.

Jenner, Henry (1904). *A Handbook of the Cornish Language*. London, D. Nutt. New edition (2010) Cathair na Mart, Evertype.

John, Catherine Rachel (1981). *The Saints of Cornwall*. Redruth, Dyllansow Truran.

Jones, Gwyn, and Thomas Jones (1949). *The Mabinogion*. London, J. M. Dent.

Jones, Kelvin I. (ed) (1996). *Cornish Fairy Folk*. Penzance, Oakmagic.

Kennedy, Patrick (1891). *Legendary Fictions of the Irish Celts*. London, Macmillan. Reprint (1998), Felinfach, Llanerch Press.

Kent, Alan M. (1991). *Clay*, Launceston: Amigo.

Kent, Alan M. (2000). *The Literature of Cornwall: Continuity, Identity, Difference, 1000–2000*. Bristol, Redcliffe Press.

Kent, Alan M. (2005). *Proper Job, Charlie Curnow!*, Wellington: Halsgrove, 2005.

Kent, Alan M. (2010). *The Theatre of Cornwall: Space, Place, Performance*. Bristol: Redcliffe.

Kent, Alan M. (2012). *Voog's Ocean*, Wellinton: Halsgrove.

Kinsella, Thomas (1970). *The Táin*. Oxford, Oxford University Press/Dolmen.

Kristeva, Julia (1989). *Black Sun*. New York, Columbia University Press.

Laming, Annette (1959). *Lascaux. Paintings and Engravings*. Harmondsworth, Penguin.

Laplanche, Jean, and Jean-Bertrand Pontalis (1988). *The Language of Psychoanalysis*. London, Karnac Books and the Institute of Psychoanalysis.

Leggat, Peter Ogilvie, and Denise V. Leggat (1987). *The Healing Wells: Cornish Cults and Customs*. Redruth, Truran

Lönnrot, Elias (1989). *The Kalevala*. Trans Keith Bosley. Oxford, Oxford University Press.

Loomis, Roger Sherman (ed) (1959). *Arthurian Literature in the Middle Ages*. Oxford, Clarendon Press.

Lynch, Frances (1970). *Prehistoric Anglesey*. Anglesey.

BIBLIOGRAPHY

McMahon, Brendan (2006). *The Princess who Ate People.* Wymeswold, Heart of Albion Press.

McMahon, Brendan (2009). *Cornish Folklore: The Nineteenth Century Background.* An Baner Kernewek.

MacCana, Proinsias (1968). *Celtic Mythology.* Reprinted (1996), London, Chancellor Press.

Mackenzie, Donald A. (1915). *Myths of Babylonia and Assyria.* London, Gresham.

MacKillop, James (1998). *Dictionary of Celtic Mythology.* Oxford, Oxford University Press.

Malinowski, Bronisław (1926). "The Role of Myth in Life" in *Psyche.*

Marks, Shula, and Peter Richardson (eds) (1984). *International Labour Migration: Historical Perspectives.* Hounslow, Maurice Temple-Smith/ University of London.

Marris, Peter (1974). *Loss and Change, Reports of the Institute of Community Studies.* London, Routledge and Kegan Paul.

Marwick, Ernest W. (2000). *The Folklore of Orkney and Shetland.* Edinburgh, Birlinn.

Masson, Jeffrey M. (1985). *The Complete Letters of Sigmund Freud to Wilhelm Fliess 1887–1904.* Cambridge Ma, Harvard University Press.

Moore, A. W. (1891). *The Folklore of the Isle of Man.* Reprinted (1991), Llanerch.

Morrison, Sophia (1911). *Manx Fairy Tales.* London, David Nutt. Reprint (1971), Douglas, Manx Museum and National Trust.

Murdoch, Brian (1993). *Cornish Literature.* Cambridge, D. S. Brewer.

Murray Parkes, Colin (1972). *Bereavement: Studies of Grief in Adult Life.* London, Tavistock Publications. Reprint (1972), Harmondsworth, Penguin.

Nance, Robert Morton (1924). *Folk-lore Recorded in the Cornish Language (1924).* 91st Annual Report of the Royal Cornwall Polytechnic Society, the author. Reprint (2000), Penzance, Oakmagic.

Nance, Robert Morton, and A. S. D. Smith (eds) (1966). *St Meriasek in Cornwall (Beunans Meriasek).* The Federation of Old Cornwall Societies.

Nicholson, Lewis E. (1963). *An Anthology of Beowulf Criticism.* Notre Dame, University of Notre Dame Press.

Norris, Edwin (1859). *The Ancient Cornish Drama.* Oxford, Oxford University Press.

Ó Cróinín, Dáibhí (2011). *Whitley Stokes 1830-1909. The Lost Celtic Notebooks Re-discovered.* Dublin. Four Courts Press.

Padel, Oliver J. (1975). *The Cornish Writings of the Boson Family.* Redruth, Institute of Cornish Studies.

Pascoe, W. H. (1985). *Teudar: A King of Cornwall.* Redruth, Truran.

Payton, Philip (1992). *The Making of Modern Cornwall: Historical Experience and the Persistence of Difference.* Redruth, Dyllansow Truran.

Payton, Philip (1996). *Cornwall.* Fowey, Alexander Associates. Revised edition (2004). *Cornwall: A History.* Fowey, Cornwall Editions.

Brendon, Piers (1975). *Hawker of Morwenstowe*. London, Cape.

Punter, David (1980). *The Literature of Terror*. London, Longman.

Purkiss, Diane (2000). *Troublesome Things: A History of Fairies and Fairy Stories*. London, Allen Lane. Reprinted (2007) as: *Fairies and Fairy Stories: A History*, London, Tempus Publishing.

Rappoport, Angelo S. (1928). *The Sea: Myths and Legends*. Reprinted (1995), London, Senate.

Rhys, John (1901). *Celtic Folklore, Volume 1: Welsh and Manx*. Oxford, Clarendon Press. Reprint (1980), London, Wildwood.

Rolt, L. T. C. (1970). *Victorian Engineering*. London, Allen Lane.

Rowe, John (1953). *Cornwall in the Age of the Industrial Revolution*. Liverpool, Liverpool University Press.

Rowse, A. L. (1941). *Tudor Cornwall: Portrait of a Society*. London, Jonathon Cape.

Rowse, A. L. (1986). *The Little Land of Cornwall*. London, Alan Sutton.

Saunders, Tim (1991). *The Wheel: An Anthology of Modern Poetry in Cornish 1850–1980*. London, Francis Boutle.

Schacker, Jennifer (2003). *National Dreams*. Philadelphia, University of Pennsylvania Press.

Seddon, Richard (1990). *The Mystery of Arthur at Tintagel*. London, Rudolf Steiner Press.

Simpson, Jacqueline, and Steve Roud (2000). *A Dictionary of English Folklore*. Oxford, Oxford University Press.

Spence, Lewis (1937). *Legendary London: Early London in Tradition and History*. London, Robert Hale and Co.

Spence, Lewis (1948). *The Minor Traditions of British Mythology*. London, Rider and Co.

Spence, Lewis (undated). *Legends and Romances of Brittany*. Reprinted (1997), New York, Dover.

Spooner, Barbara (1965). "The Giants of Cornwall" in *Folklore*. 76, §6–32.

Stern, Stephen, and John A. Cicala (eds) (1991). *Creative Ethnicity: Symbols and Strategies of Contemporary Ethnic Life*. Logan, Utah, Utah State University Press.

Stevens, Frank Leonard (1928). *Through Merrie England: The Pageantry and Pastimes of the Village and the Town*. London, Frederick Warne.

Stokes, Whitley (1864). *Guireans an bys. The Creation of the World*. London, Williams and Norgate.

Stokes, Whitley (1872). *The Life of St Meriasek, Bishop and Confessor*. London, Trübner.

Stoyle, Mark (2002). *West Britons: Cornish Identities and the Early Modern British State*. Exeter, University of Exeter.

Stoyle, Mark (2005). *Soldiers and Strangers: An Ethnic History of the English Civil War*.

BIBLIOGRAPHY

Strachey, James (ed) (1917). *Complete Psychological Works of Sigmund Freud.* London, Hogarth Press.

Thomas, C. (1997). *See your own Country First: The Geography of a Railway Landscape.*

Thomas, Graham, and Nicholas Williams (eds) (2007). *Bewnans Ke: The Life of St Kea.* Exeter, University of Exeter Press.

Tomlin, E. W. F. (1982). *In Search of St Piran.* Padstow, Lodenek

Traill, David A. (1995). *Schliemann of Troy: Treasure and Deceit.* London, Penguin.

Warner, Marina (1994). *From the Beast to the Blond.* London, Chatto and Windus.

Westland, Ella (1997). *Cornwall: The Cultural Construction of Place.* Penzance, Patten Press/University of Exeter.

Westwood, Jennifer (1987). *Albion: A Guide to Legendary Britain.* London, Paladin.

Westwood, Jennifer, and Jacqueline Simpson (2005). *The Lore of the Land.* London, Penguin.

Whetter, James (1988). *The History of Glasney College.* Padstow, Tabb House.

White, James F. (1962). *The Cambridge Movement: The Ecclesiologists and the Gothic Revival.* Cambridge, Cambridge University Press.

Wicker, Brian (1975). *The Story-Shaped World: Fiction and Metaphysics.* London, Athlone Press.

Williams, Derek R. (ed) (2004). *Henry and Katharine Jenner: A Celebration of Cornwall's Culture, Language and Identity.* London, Francis Boutle.

Williams, Nicholas. (1995) *Cornish Today: An examination of the revived language.* Sutton Coldfield: Kernewek dre Lyther. Third edition (2006) Cathair na Mart, Evertype.

Williams, Nicholas. (2006a) *Writings on Revived Cornish.* Cathair na Mart, Evertype.

Williams, Nicholas. (2006b) *Towards Authentic Cornish.* Cathair na Mart, Evertype.

Woodhouse, Harry (2002). *The Cornish Passion Poem in Facsimile.* Gareth Kennow.

Zaczek, Iain (2005). *Fairy Art, Artists and Inspirations.* London, Starfire Publishing.

Zimmermann, Georges Denis (2001). *The Irish Storyteller.* Dublin, Four Courts Press.

Zipes, Jack (ed) (2001). *The Oxford Companion to Fairy Tales.* Oxford, Oxford University Press.

Žižek, Slavoj (2008). *In Defence of Lost Causes.* London, Verso.

Index

Lightning Source UK Ltd.
Milton Keynes UK
UKOW04f1051040917
308543UK00001B/11/P